T0129679

Awaken
and Stir Up the Gift of Love

ELNORA WILSON

WESTBOW
PRESS®
A DIVISION OF THOMAS NELSON
& ZONDERVAN

WestBow Press books may be ordered through booksellers or by contacting:

WestBow Press
A Division of Thomas Nelson & Zondervan
1663 Liberty Drive
Bloomington, IN 47403
www.westbowpress.com
1 (866) 928-1240

Scripture taken from the King James Version of the Bible.

ISBN: 978-1-9736-0396-2 (sc)
ISBN: 978-1-9736-0397-9 (hc)
ISBN: 978-1-9736-0395-5 (e)

Library of Congress Control Number: 2017914149

Print information available on the last page.

WestBow Press rev. date: 12/11/2017

Contents

Preface

The purpose of this book is to spiritually challenge the body of Christ to seek God for spiritual maturity—not through the evaluation of others but in self-evaluation. Jesus has given man one primary commandment for edifying the kingdom of God. This commandment single-handedly puts all the others in perspective. Without being condescending to another person's self-worth, he shows the world to whom the saints belong. There is no greater method of communicating selflessness than in the actions of agape. Agape is a kind of love that affects life more deeply than any circumstantial emotion that comes and goes based on a given situation. God gave his only Son for man's sake to demonstrate the effectiveness of love. This unconditional love is the standard God used to identify Christians with the body of Christ.

Love is such a powerful tool that it makes a person love those who are hateful. Love doesn't scourge a person for falling into sin; instead, it will overpower evil and do the one thing that it does best: love. Unfortunately, too many saints focus on the alternative and practice those things that are unkind. Perhaps cruelty might be a more precise word. Compassion is quite difficult for many Christians, whereas Jesus showed empathy before he came in the flesh, during his stay on earth, and after he returned to glory. Christians also find it hard to pray for certain people, but Jesus, the Great I AM, prayed for those for whom he died. God, in the second person of the Trinity, kneeled down on his knees to pray for people. So the question is: who do we think we are? Jesus even prayed for those who put him on the cross. Is there a significant reason why some Christians fail to pray for their enemies or people who hurt them? Do they proclaim to be better than the

Almighty? Or are they trapped in the old man's mind-set? The power of love resides in every child of God, and therefore it must be displayed.

In spite of the cost for his ransom, in spite the pain of being separated from his Father, and in spite of the suffering and the shame, love sacrificed it all to reconcile man back to himself. He became the perfect example for Christians to mimic. This book is a challenge for all Christians to look in the mirror (the Holy Bible) in order to see what the Spirit has to say and then make the necessary changes to mature in Christ.

Introduction

Who Am I?

Is mankind capable of loving based on the standards of God? Is the human mind equipped to love those who hate us or those who purposely hurt us? Knowing who we are in Christ makes it possible. The Bible makes our true identities quite clear; therefore, we should study the word of God to identify with him.

The Bible teaches that man and woman are living souls, unlike animals and other living things. Genesis gives an account of the origin of humankind and our unique likeness to the image of God:

> God created man in his own image, in the image of God created he him; male and female created he them. (Gen. 1:27)

> And the LORD God formed man of the dust of the ground, and breathed into his nostrils the breath of life; and man became a living soul. (Gen. 2:7)

> The LORD God caused a deep sleep to fall upon Adam ... and he took one of his ribs ... made he a woman. (Gen. 2:21–22)

Therefore, Adam named her *woman* because she was taken out of man. The identities of man and woman came from God. For this reason, this foundation shouldn't be confused with feelings, emotions, or preferences.

The human body consists of mind, body, and soul/spirit. Psychologists in their scientific studies have classified humans into four behavior types: type A (aggressive/competitive/uncompassionate), type B (enthusiastic/procrastinator/impatient), type C (meticulous/controller/antisocial), and type D (organized/compassionate/anxiety). These are said to be the categories of individual mental functions. This theory doesn't align with the characteristics of a person who is identified with Christ. Certainly, everyone has traits belonging to one or more of these behavior types, but to put them into a category for self-definition causes a conflict with the Creator. There are other studies that suggest humans have the same characteristics as animals, once again attempting to link humankind to the theory of evolution. Evolutionists classify humans as Homo sapiens, insinuating that humankind is a modern ape, which goes against the word of God. The Bible specifically says, "Let us make man in our image," in opposition to the theory of evolution. *Us* in this text gives reference to God, to the Word of God (Jesus's original form), and to the Spirit of God.

To answer the question "Who am I?" requires a spiritual response. The soul of humankind is the breath of God, and therefore it can't ever die. "So when this corruptible shall have put on incorruption, and this mortal shall have put on immortality" (1 Cor. 15:54), those who have answered the holy call will return to him. Answering the call means accepting the responsibility of the call by living life in a new perspective. Paul defines it perfectly in Galatians 2:20: "I am crucified with Christ: nevertheless I live; yet not I, but Christ liveth in me: and the life which I now live in the flesh I live by the faith of the Son of God, who loved me, and gave himself for me." Paul went a little further in Romans 8 to say those who have answered the call are no longer defined by the flesh, but by the Spirit.

> Therefore if any man be in Christ, he is a new creature: old things are passed away; behold, all things are become new. (2 Cor. 5:17)

Ye are a chosen generation, a royal priesthood, an holy
nation, a peculiar people: that ye should shew forth the
praises of him who hath called you out of darkness into
his marvelous light. (1 Pet. 2:9)

God, who hath reconciled us to himself by Jesus Christ,
and hath given to us the ministry of reconciliation. (2
Cor. 5:18)

Now then we are ambassadors for Christ. (2 Cor. 5:20)

That's who we are, which makes us more than capable of loving
those who seem unlovable. The indwelling power of God also gives
saints the strength and the will to obey his word, which allows love to
express itself. Knowing our identities in Christ is part of revealing the
gift of love.

Chapter 1

Awaken

After a long, hard day of work, there's nothing like a good night's sleep. Waking up the next morning revived and refreshed makes starting a new day more energetic. Failing to awaken physically signifies that the body no longer has life in it. Conversely, for the body to arise without the zeal of God implies the absence of spiritual life, whether it's a dead man walking or someone sleepwalking. The difference in these two groups of people is revealed in their spiritual status. A dead man walking has never known Jesus as Lord; therefore, he is considered a sinner who is destined for hell, unless he confesses hope in Christ. People who are sleepwalking were once eager to serve the Lord, but somewhere along the way circumstances, materialism, or deception distorted their vision. This can lead to operating as the rest of the world, not denying Christ but merely being caught up.

> God is waiting for those who are called by his name to turn from their wicked ways.

It's time to awaken; nap time is over. The Bible teaches us to be watchful of Jesus's coming. "But of that day and that hour knoweth no man, no, not the angels which are in heaven, neither the Son, but the Father" (Mark 13:32). Being asleep is a state of unconsciousness, which implies being out of fellowship with God. There's no will to obey the word of God when the relationship is disconnected. No man can be a servant of God in darkness. Those who are on the alert must show love toward fellow Christians who have lost their way. To be spiritually asleep in a way is like taking sleeping pills. Ambien and Lunesta are prescription medications used to help people fall asleep quickly and remain asleep for seven to eight hours. Once a deep sleep has taken over the body, it needs to remain asleep in order to function properly the next day. If not, there's fatigue and a lack of full alertness. Being out of fellowship with Christ makes it impossible to be Christ-like. Without the power of God working within us, falling into a state of carelessness is probable. Spiritual negligence puts the flesh in charge, resulting in all sorts of sins that the mind feels obligated to justify. Mark 13 warns of Jesus coming and finding some asleep. "[Therefore, he says] what I say unto you I say unto all, Watch" (Mark 13:37).

There's nothing positive about sleepwalking. Too often the "sleepwalking club" manages to keep the group together by congregating to discuss things of darkness. Perhaps doing this helps them feel comfortable because it relates to their current spiritual states. To awaken from your deep sleep, you must first acknowledge that you are operating in darkness. Seeing sin for what it is and not what you want it to be is a sign of awakening. Pray to God for deliverance and believe he will answer. Not only believe, but also step out on faith, knowing that he is more than capable of doing what he says. Not only step out on faith, but walk victoriously. "We are more than conquerors" (Rom. 8:37). Wake up from unproductivity and begin a good work for the Lord, "knowing the time, that now it is high time to awake out of sleep: for now is our salvation nearer than when we believed" (Rom. 13:11). The time is drawing near, and even Jesus said, "I must work the works of him that sent me, while it is day: the night cometh, when no man can work" (John 9:4).

Why reject wisdom? Jesus said through Paul's writing that his coming is near. So, wake up! Our salvation is closer than we think, so wake up from sin and begin walking in righteousness for his name's sake.

Making a conscious decision requires being alert. When a person is passed out, it is impossible to be mindful of surrounding activities. Consequently, unrighteousness is at work full time, leading its victim down a path that could be terminal. People fail to see the dangers of being out of fellowship with God, especially those in the church. "Once saved, always saved" isn't a key to the kingdom of heaven. "Once saved" is the bond between man and God by way of the Holy Spirit that only requires one true union. "Always saved" is the assurance from God of predestination resulting in a real relationship between God and humans. To assume that accepting hope in Christ allows careless living is evidence of a person who has not met God. This is not to say that a person can't fall or get caught up in a particular sin. Perhaps it wasn't done intentionally. David is a perfect example of falling into sin. When he was caught up by Bathsheba's beauty, he became consumed by his lust for her. But God sent Nathan to give David the opportunity to see himself. When David received the conviction, the Bible says that David replied, "I have sinned against the LORD" (2 Sam. 12:13). According to *Matthew Henry's Commentary on the Whole Bible*, "God may suffer his people to fall into sin, and to lie a great while in it, yet he will, by some means or other, recover them to repentance, bring them to himself and to their right mind again (Henry, 1991).

"Not being in his right mind" in the text suggests that he was temporarily disconnected from his relationship with God. In Psalm 51, David sincerely and compassionately repents of his sin and begs God for forgiveness. This psalm shows that God is merciful and forgiving when a person is truly sorry. Conversely, those who feel that being saved gives them the freedom to sin really mean they are free from righteousness. Christianity isn't a religion; it's a lifestyle. Neither does it legalize sin. Sinners are not subject to obeying the word of God because they are not his. Those who are his but have fallen back into sin, receive the mercies of God that give us the opportunity to repent. Thinking back to our childhoods, our parents would call for us to get out of bed for school. But we were sleeping so well and the bed was so warm that we couldn't hear the call. Well, the longer they called, the louder they got. After a while, they'd come into the room and shake us. How many of us is God shaking, and yet we still have one eye closed?

As long as the enemy can keep you from operating in your true identity, he can keep you from being free. Being spiritually asleep won't allow you to perform based on who you are in Christ. This frame of mind is known as being delusional. Have you ever been in a deep sleep and suddenly awakened by something? For a moment, you don't know what's going on. You have to compose yourself to get a handle of things.

The delusional Christian goes to church every Sunday with church clothes on (occasionally worldly attire is justified because the mind is not fully awakened), sings in the choir, teaches Sunday school, ushers, and even preaches with a false impression. God is not pleased with such performances. He has people in the congregation seeking divine help, but many leaders in the church are misrepresenting Christ. A performance is merely putting on a show but lacks the anointing. After a long week of dealing with the circumstances of life, we long for Sunday morning so we may be among other Christians. You've prayed, and your spirit is full of song and praises to the Lord, but you walk in the local assembly to find people feeling worse than you. Some are selfish, others have an attitude, and a few are showing off their new outfits. So, what do we do in these types of situations? We pray for one another, instead of placing judgment. It is good to be spiritually prepared to worship. It is also a perfect place to intercede for those who may not be as spiritually mature as you are or for those who may have one eye closed.

It's not always easy to be a Christian. The challenge of giving a helping hand to those who believe that being asleep is okay, while dealing with your own problems, makes some days more difficult than others. Believe it or not, this is a good place for God to take us to a higher level. It's not pleasant to teach the unteachable or encourage those who don't want to be encouraged. Neither is it pleasant to maintain a smile when those you are ministering to are throwing stones at you. This road of righteousness requires a personal relationship with Christ. Christians can't stand alone because the flesh will surface, resulting in an act of ungodliness. Jesus knows firsthand what it takes to make this stand. "Father, if thou be willing, remove this cup from me" (Luke 22:42). Jesus was fully man and God; therefore, the agony he would endure in the flesh briefly concerned him, but in the Spirit, he didn't want to be separated from his Father. Considering the heart of Jesus, can you hear him saying he is here to save you, not hurt you? He's saying the path you're on will condemn your soul; so, let him help you. You can't see it, but there is an evil spirit out to destroy you. Jesus didn't respond to evil spirits by what he felt, but by what he knew. He is the perfect example for us. People will hurt us, lie to us, kill us with their tongues, and scandalize our names. In these instances, we must respond based on what we know, not our feelings. They can't see it, but we can. Therefore, let us stay focused on our mission. Chapter one of 2 Peter makes mention of Christian virtues. "But he that lacketh these things is blind, and cannot see afar off, and hath forgotten that he was purged from his old sins. Wherefore the rather, brethren, give diligence to make your calling and election sure" (2 Pet. 1:9–10). Those who are persistent in the Christian walk of faith must pray for those who have lost their way, regardless of how aggravated they may become. It's not our place to force the Bible on anyone, but when the opportunity presents itself, we should be ready to share. Furthermore, we can always pray for people without their knowledge. We don't have to get in a person's face to witness; we merely have to talk with God about a broken person and let him handle it.

Persistence is necessary to reach those who have grown tired. Although God will not put more on his children than we can bear, the Christian journey can be hard for those who are not grounded in his word. It can also be tiresome when there isn't a close relationship with Christ. From a realistic perspective, working in the local assembly can war against those who are dedicated, when those who fail to work complain about the way things are being done. In many cases, the same people are holding positions in most auxiliaries because too many individuals are merely churchgoers and not working out their salvations, as scripture teaches in Philippians 2:12. Therefore, handling church affairs, working in different ministries, ministering to the lost, encouraging those who are weak, and other responsibilities can often make the cross seem unbearable.

Consider moving into a new house or an apartment. Initially during the packing process, everything is wrapped properly and placed in a labeled box. On the other hand, packing consistently without a break to rest or eat can change the mind-set. "Let's just put them in a box and deal with it later." This means it may or may not be wrapped. But if there are rest periods throughout the day with meals and a few snacks, by the end of the day, the mind-set will be the same as it started. Why? Can you see our spiritual walk in this same perspective? As new Christians, we are on fire for the Lord. Unfortunately, many of us grow tired because we are not feeding our spirits daily; some people only receive spiritual nourishment once a week. We shouldn't expect much from these Christians or waste a lot of time complaining about their lack of service. Many Christians never take the time to rest in the Lord by meditating on his word, which authorizes his truth to work in the soul. Fellowship is also important to encourage one another in love by assembling ourselves together with other saints (Heb. 10:25). During the gathering, God can be highly lifted up and glorified as the saints come together in unity to magnify his name. No matter what we do in life, it's all to the glory of God; therefore, we can't look through our physical eyes because we'll always grow tired, perhaps even exhausted. The Christian journey is solely spiritual, working through the physical body. Staying focused is the key. Encouraging those who have lost their way or have grown weary is only part of our calling. Witnessing is witnessing, whether it's to a sinner or to a backslider; God has no prospective persons, and neither should we. He loves everyone, and his word teaches that we should too.

Must Jesus bear the cross alone and all the world go free? "If any man will come after me, let him deny himself, and take up his cross, and follow me" (Matt. 16:24).

Chapter 2

Stir Up the Gift of Love

"Repent, and be baptized every one of you in the name of Jesus Christ for the remission of sins, and ye shall receive the gift of the Holy Ghost" (Acts 2:38). The gift of the Holy Spirit is the true gift that is God taking residence in the body, referred to as the temple. "Know ye not that your body is the temple of the Holy Spirit which is in you" (1 Cor. 6:19). Who is this Spirit living in you? First, he is the third person of the Trinity. Second, he is the link between God and humans. He's also our intercessor and comforter. Therefore, when we pray to God, this indwelling Spirit of God is talking with himself in us. Our physical bodies are incapable of communicating with him spiritually. Although our souls are eternal, they are still finite in comparison to the infinite God. It is by the magnificent gift of the Holy Spirit that we can function in his fruit, which is love, joy, peace, long-suffering, gentleness, goodness, faith, meekness, and temperance. Notice there are ten fruits listed in scripture, but they take on the singular form. These characteristics help define who he is; just as the human heart has four major parts, it is still only one heart. Finally, he is the Spirit of truth. He is the only absolute truth who has come as the Comforter. "When he the Spirit of truth, is come, he will guide you into the truth" (John 16:13). Why is he a gift? He is a gift because we simply cannot earn those things he has to offer. In other words, neither he nor his gift are for sale. No one could afford them even if they were for sale. His gift is intangible and therefore not purchasable. He has many attributes, of which some are accessible to humans, such as the fruit of the Spirit. Others are not—for instance, his omnipotence, omniscience, omnipresence, and sovereignty.

The gift of the Spirit of God is given by God to anyone who accepts the holy call. Operating at a higher level in the Spirit is fulfilled by one's relationship with God. Natural talents are given by God to everyone at birth. Thousands of people who may or may not be Christians perform their talents daily. The ability to sing, swim, teach, speak, work well with your hands, and more are God-given. Certain careers require special people due to the temperament of the job. Not everyone can be a surgeon, many can't handle being a mortician, and most don't want to be an autopsy pathologist. There are other special talents that God has not given to the average person to deal with on a daily basis. Spiritual talents consisting of compassion, discerning of spirits, pastoring, faithfulness, and speaking in tongues are unique gifts. People are talented in many ways, but it's not enough to have the gifts; God expects us to utilize them to his glorification.

Complacency hinders the will to learn more about Christ. This can cause a lack of relationship to possibly lead individuals to eventually question their salvation. To merely say, "I am saved," with no desire to grow in the relationship leaves room for uncertainty. It's easy to fall when your spirit is weak. Daily repentance is necessary to renew the right spirit and maintain a good relationship with God. This type of renewal doesn't come from listening to the Bible on a phone, a CD, or an iPod player. This is fine in passing, but growth comes from self-effort. Riding in your car, exercising, and sitting at your desk are great opportunities for listening to the word of God. But we can't dissect a scripture by listening to someone read it. Studying requires biblically defining words to acquire wisdom, knowledge, and understanding, which leads to spiritual growth. Once a person is willing to apply what God has said, then comes the time to stir up the gift.

The Holy Ghost can move freely in those of us who allow Jesus to reign in our lives. Let's stir up the gift of God's indwelling power. In order to reach this power, we must change our mind-set from the physical to the spiritual and reflect on the elements of his supremacy. The sovereignty of God is unlimited. For instance, it is his power that keeps everything working simultaneously. The sun is still burning in place, the moon still gives light at night, the planets are still in perfect orbit, and the stars have not fallen to destroy the earth. In addition, his miraculous power has created and controls the function of our unique anatomy systems. In detail, he designed and fashioned the muscular, cardiovascular, skeletal, nervous, reproductive, urinary, endocrine, lymphatic, and digestive systems to balance our body's daily operations. His power is more than we can possibly envision. By his own might, he implanted himself in a woman, raised Lazarus from the dead, and healed the sick. It is in his power that we live, move, and have our being. Our spiritual gifts are empowered by this very same God; therefore, we should be grateful for the privilege of sharing our wonderful God with the world. This power is not capable of failing. It will not force its abilities on us. We have to seek after it, and then it will work through us.

"It is more blessed to give than to receive" (Acts 20:35). This text initially leads most people to think of money or material things, but the greatest gift of giving is of oneself. We all have special gifts, which are not necessarily for monetary profit. It could possibly be a call to service. Everyone with the gift of singing isn't called to record music, but rather to bless those in the local assembly or the community. The church needs counselors, lawyers, secretaries, custodians, accountants, and many other professions where people have gifts to share. Giving with love also refers to gifts of patience, tolerance, compassion, being cheerful, having a pleasant smile, and embracing others. A person shouldn't have to be married to experience love. Being loved by someone regardless of financial status or popularity is demonstrating love in its most genuine form. Being generous with those less fortunate is great, but let us share those inner gifts that people can carry with them wherever they go. If compassion isn't your particular gift, it doesn't mean you can't share it, but it does mean you need more practice.

Stir up the gift of agape. There are many things and characteristics that make a person unique. The whole world is distinctively and wonderfully made. Emotion is a characteristic distinctly selected and rightly rooted in the soul of mankind. Although we are different, there is one thing that humans have in common: a longing for love. In spite of educational status, success in life, family size, poverty level, or social status, we all long for it—even celebrities. An effectual spirit such as this is designed to work through the hearts of all of us who have breath in our bodies. But how many people truly possess it? How many people actually share it with others? Unfortunately, people fail to see the value of this beautiful, magnificent thing called love existing in four different forms to meet the needs of mind, body, and soul. A love between friends (philia), the sexual passions of love between man and woman (eros), parental love (storge), and unconditional love (agape) work in unison in a unique way.

The Bible teaches a husband to love his wife as Christ loves the church, which he died for, and it teaches wives to submit themselves to their own husbands (Eph. 5:22, 25). Neither should they withhold sexual relations from one another (1 Cor. 7:5). Second, the Bible tells parents to train up their children in the way they should go, and in love to not spare the rod (Prov. 22:6; Prov. 13:24). Third, a true friend is rare. The Bible says that a friend loves at all times, and in order to have a friend, we must show ourselves friendly (Prov. 17:17; Prov. 18:24). Finally, God teaches the saints to love one another to fulfill the needs of the church (John 13:34; Rom. 13:8–14). This text also teaches that upholding the law is fulfilling the law. People shouldn't deliberately set out to hurt loved ones when the love of Christ dwells within them. The text goes on to say that "it is high time to awake out of sleep." This kind of sleep isn't pertaining to awakening from a good night's rest to start a new day for school or work. It's giving reference to a spiritual awakening in regard to salvation.

Jesus is passionate about people loving one another, because that's who he is (1 John 4:8, 16). If we are the children of God, it is our place to resemble him. It doesn't matter how different people may be; the one thing we all desire is to be loved. Some respond to life negatively because no one has shown love toward them. Some people have committed murder, because a spouse has broken vows in the love relationship. Many youths have joined gangs in search of it. Females give their bodies away, trying to find it, because it wasn't given to them at home or they failed to see it. Lesbians are seeking love in unnatural affections because they can't find it in men. Love is sometimes so desired that people are looking for it but don't really know what they are in search of. The end to this search is in Jesus Christ. God is love, and once he is living within you, it is available to share with others. Unfortunately, in the minds of many, it is better to deny the existence of love than to search for it and never find it. Therefore, it is high time for the saints of God to stir up the gifts of love.

What is agape? It is the Greek word for love. It will stand no matter what comes.

> Love [agape] suffereth long, and is kind; love envieth not; love vaunteth [boast] not itself, it is not puffed up, Doth not behave itself unseemly, seeketh not her own, is not easily provoked, thinketh no evil; Rejoiceth not in iniquity, but rejoiceth in the truth; Beareth all things, believeth all things, hopeth all things, endureth all things. Love never faileth." (1 Cor. 13:4–8)

What a challenge! This love isn't something that can be achieved on one's own, but only through the presence of Jesus Christ. The self will always get in the way when we independently try to express this attribute without its source. Why did the text refer to love as "her" when it said "seeketh not her own?" Love has many gifts within itself, making it effective in more ways than one. Love will give birth to as many gifts as one person is willing to share. Long-suffering alone will disqualify many because we are a "right now" group of people. The capacity for "enduring all things" disqualifies the rest of us because most of us have too much pride to endure certain things or too much shame over what people may say.

So, where is the love? The way we can handle shame and pride is by putting on the shield of faith to stop the painful words that the enemy uses to prevent love from going forth (Eph. 6:15). Let us stir up the gift to eliminate envy, get rid of pride, destroy rudeness and distasteful words and conduct, leave selfishness behind, maintain self-control, and turn from evil deeds. Once we let Jesus reign in us, we can honestly pray for God to bless others, be hopeful instead of negative, live in the faith that God can do what he says in his word, and bear the cross of Jesus. The exceptional genius of agape guides the other three types of love to function in its proper place. Although operating in this gift may seem impossible, it's not. We simply have to do what has hindered Christians from the beginning: deny the self.

> For all that is in the world, the lust of the flesh, and the lust of the eyes, and the pride of life, is not of the Father, but is of the world." (1 John 2:16)

> This I say then, Walk in the Spirit, and ye shall not fulfill the lust of the flesh. (Gal. 5:16)

Stir up the gift of peace. "Peace I leave with you, my peace I give unto you" (John 14:27). To whose peace is this text referring? The text is referring to Jesus. He is the only source of peace because he is peace (Isa. 9:6). In each saint lies the gift of peace, which may or may not be active depending on whether its presence is acknowledged. It's there, but it can only be activated when it is stirred up. How can the gift of peace be awakened from its sleep to God's glorification? We can stir up peace by making it alive within us by letting "the peace of God rule in your hearts" (Col. 3:15). You may be wondering how to acquire the peace of God. The Bible teaches:

> Rejoice in the Lord alway: and again I say, Rejoice. Let your moderation be known unto all men. The Lord is at hand. Be careful for nothing; but in every thing by prayer and supplication with thanksgiving let your requests be made known unto God. And the *peace of God,* which passeth all understanding, shall keep your hearts and minds through Christ Jesus. (Phil. 4:4–7; emphasis added)

There is nothing like being at peace with God. There's a calmness that can't be explained. Although circumstances may be hard to manage, God's peace has the power to take us through them with a smile. Spiritual gifts are beneficial to both the Christian and those witnessing the gift.

The people around us need to see us at peace even when our world is falling apart. This isn't to say that we can't mourn or express our emotions, but it does mean that we should handle tests and trials differently from the world. It is important to reveal Christ at all times in order to help spark those who are asleep, and to draw people who are looking for direction in life who may be filled with uncertainties. It is our duty as representatives of Christ to be obedient to his word. When we fail to take advantage of operating under his wonderful benefits, people living in spiritual darkness remain in darkness. Those asleep are merely turning over in their spiritual beds to find a more comfortable position. The devil uses vulnerable-minded people to bring confusion in the body of Christ. God knows that we are being attacked every day by the enemy turning us against one another. Satan uses different personalities and characteristics to set traps for God's children. Sometimes we allow him to makes us an enemy to ourselves. The Bible is teaching us to live peaceably with them in spite of who they are, so that they may see who we are. This spiritual journey can be hard at times, so in order to be at peace in the evil day, God says to have "your feet shod with the preparation of the gospel of peace" (Eph. 6:15). The purpose of having your feet shod is to walk in the gospel, which prepares us to face evil. When we anticipate rain, normally we'll get an umbrella. When the teacher announces a test will be given, we prepare by studying. God says the enemy walks about as a roaring lion, seeking whom he can destroy. Therefore, we prepare by putting on our spiritual shoes because it is evident that the evil one is awaiting the opportunity to strike. Let us be ready when he comes on our jobs, in our homes, in the store, or in the local assembly.

Satan comes to steal our peace. He sets his plan in motion through anyone who will make themselves available. Some people feel that they are above being used by the devil. They become attached to titles or positions and forget that we are in a spiritual battle. No one is exempt from the deceitful manipulation of Satan—not pastors, preachers, deacons, teachers, or their wives. Consider ships in a body of stormy waters. The water doesn't say to one ship, "Oh, look at the beautiful colors. I won't press against you." Or, "This is an old ship. I'll press harder against you." Neither will it say, "Because you are a more expensive ship, I won't bother you." The water really has no control over how it presses against the ships, or how it may cover them. It is driven by wind and energy. Evil forces have no power unless people give those powers life. Satan as the wind and energy is forcefully pushing us (water), but if we resist him, peace will reside. Have you ever witnessed a calm sea under a bright blue sky? There's nothing like it. Christians mustn't give the devil room to work through us. He has this charismatic way of taking a bad situation and making the motive appear positive.

For example, a misunderstanding (initiated by Satan) can ruin a person's reputation in the local assembly. Let's say a single female consults a married woman about an issue on her job concerning a male co-worker, but the married woman hears, "She has a thing for my husband. That's why she came to me." After the conversation is complete, due to her Good Samaritan work in the church, the married woman feels compelled to warn other wives to keep an eye on the single woman when she's around their husbands. Satan's plan has taken root and has produced offspring. It's like investing and letting your money work for you. Satan sets the trap and then sits back to watch God's people carry out his plan. This is a worldwide issue because Satan is all around the world. We have to start thinking bigger and praying for the body of Christ, not just those around us. If you have been a victim of slander, put your spiritual shoes on. The only thing that really matters is what God thinks. If he is okay with who you are, don't be concerned about what people are saying. You can walk in peace!

The devil will keep you anxious by using people to exaggerate the truth. If you know who you are in Christ, the world won't be able to move you. Also, remain focused on things that are honest, true, just, pure, lovely, and those things of a good report for the peace of God to be with you (Phil. 4:8).

Stir up the gift of life: Jesus Christ. The most precious gift known to man is our redeemer, Jesus Christ. He came for the purpose of saving man by reconciling us back to God, to restore the communion that was once broken. Now that we have this amazing relationship with God, we have to live it so the world can see what it means to have joy on earth. Although the God of glory has come to dwell among us and we may praise him in sincere adoration, this doesn't compare to the glory we shall behold in the heavens. How do we show the world Christ? We reveal the Savior by being Christ-like. We love whom he loves, we hate what he hates, and we must stand firm on what is right. We can't be distracted by the things of this world, and neither can we allow the world to define us. Our identities have already been defined by God in heaven, and we can't forget who we are in Christ. Our fellow brothers and sisters in Christ who have fallen asleep are having nightmares but can't wake up. Their souls are tossing and turning; the battle is tearing them apart. We've got to be patient while we encourage and remind them of God's good news. "For the Lord himself shall descend from heaven with a shout, with the voice of the archangel, and with the trump of God: and the dead in Christ shall rise first: Then we which are alive and remain shall be caught up together with them in the clouds, to meet the Lord in the air: and so shall we ever be with the Lord. Wherefore comfort one another with these words" (1 Thess. 4:16–18).

There are others who sleep but have never known God because they failed to answer the call. They need us to live right for them as well. Many of them failed to confess Christ because they simply couldn't see why they should. They have money and other material possessions, but the joy of the Lord is far from them. Christians have to become fans of God. Do you know what fans do? They support celebrities or teams, following them from city to city. Fans make a lot of noise for those they support. They'll pay top dollar to attend concerts or go to games. Some people are die-hard fans, meaning events are sold out. Jesus is looking for die-hard fans mostly because he deserves it. It's also because that's what the world needs.

Romans 6:23 tells us "the gift of God is eternal life through Jesus Christ our Lord." Therefore, "Stand fast therefore in the liberty wherewith Christ hath made us free" (Gal. 5:1). Eternal freedom is evident for those who are in Christ, but the actual state of liberty begins while we are still in the flesh. In this text, Paul was talking to the Galatians' church about the bondage of legalism. He was teaching them about spiritual freedom, while they still have the mobility of their bodily functions. We have this same freedom because *"God so loved* the world, that he gave his only begotten Son, that whosoever believeth in him should not perish, but have everlasting life" (John 3:16). The word *so* emphasizes the word *loved*, suggesting that it wasn't just a word but a promise—a promise of damnation or a promise of salvation. The sanctified promises embrace the eternal blessings of God not only to Christians but also to anyone that will receive him. "For whosoever shall call upon the name of the Lord shall be saved" (Rom. 10:13). As saints, we rest on the assurance of our salvation: "ye were sealed with that Holy Spirit of promise" (Eph. 1:13). "Ye are sealed unto the day of redemption" (Eph. 4:30). "And this is the confidence that we have in him that, if we ask any thing according to his will, he heareth us" (1 John 5:14). His will is clearly mentioned in his word; therefore, it is wise to pray his word back to him. We have the right to approach God concerning his promises when we live in obedience. "If ye abide in me, and my words abide in you, ye shall ask what ye will, and it shall be done unto you" (John 14:7). He is able to take care of those that are his. "God shall supply all your need according to his riches in glory by Christ Jesus" (Phil. 4:19). Well, just how much can he supply? "The earth is the LORD's, and the fullness thereof; the world, and they that dwell therein" (Ps. 24:1).

We have this magnificent gift, which unfortunately is treated like a burden. God has given us his best; it is up to us to appreciate it. If we can only be thankful, then we can enjoy life in our temporary state as we await the eternal life. Living the Christian experience is only possible as children of God, because his Spirit lives within us. Therefore, we walk in love for all mankind. Instead, everyday it's a cliché. "Another day-another dollar. I have to get up and go to this job." "Oh, my goodness, do I have to go to school today?" "These children get on my nerves." "My husband won't give me any space." "My wife needs to know every step I take." "Why do I have to be nice to them when they are ugly to me?" We hear complaint after complaint, which isn't a form of witnessing but resisting. We have the joy of the Lord within us, so let us get excited about Jesus and tell the world about his grace and mercy. Let us live in the same love and peace God gave us through the gift of Jesus and stop expecting the world to be what it is not. We are in the light, and therefore God expects us to walk in it. The sinner can only do what he or she knows.

In order to stir up the Christian experience, we must meditate on his word, spend quality time with him in prayer, and apply godly conduct. Knowledge without application won't generate a productive joyful soul. Anyone can be happy, because it is simply an emotion that comes and goes with the drop of a hat, but joy is an inner peace. The world needs to know that circumstances don't control joy in the life of a Christian; it's merely an opportunity to grow closer to God. The closer we are to God, the more excited we can become about the gospel.

Real joy can be found as a result of those things God has done for mankind. He gave humans free will to eternal life, he has sealed Christians unto the day of redemption, he has promised never to leave nor forsake us, and he's prepared a place for his children that hasn't been seen by humans. When these truths dwell within the souls of humans, they allow the power of God to grow stronger. Staying focused assists in learning more about the promises of God, which will compel the heart to grow fonder and mature into a more joyous life. Although being at a higher spiritual level is the greatest honor, it isn't the ultimate Christian experience. Always remember that we are still in the flesh and should never let our guard down. The joy of the Lord is indeed our strength, but the devil craves to make us fall. Therefore, as we grow in Christ, it is essential to avoid situations that cause us to fall. Learn how to deal with temptations, especially those that pull at our weaknesses. Sin has a unique way of bringing guilt into existence, which could steal our joy. Those who are asleep must witness our joy to help disintegrate the strongholds in their lives.

The importance of having an understanding heart during a person's soulful perplexity is in offering encouragement. Have you ever experienced the soulful trauma after a dominating sin has awakened from its sleep? Do you feel that your relationship is so close to God that you are invincible for such things to happen to you? It doesn't matter how spiritual we are on earth; the possibility of falling into sin will eventually come in some form or fashion. As long as we dwell in an earthly body, we are subject to gossip, deception, hatred, theft, sexual sin, greed, and lust. So, let us be compassionate toward those who are dealing with unpeaceful souls. Some may question what causes a soul to be without peace. The process is simple but unfortunate. The soul retreats, or perhaps falls sleepy, once a controlling sin has awakened, allowing unrighteousness to take over the body. Instead of lofty looks and negative conversations about them (which is also a sin), we should be an inspiration. In the place of talking about them, let's talk about what God's word has said about their situation. "He restores my soul and leads me in the path of righteousness for his name sake" (Ps. 23:3). God's promises to us include his grace and mercy. His sovereignty makes it impossible for him to abandon us.

> I give unto them eternal life; and they shall never perish, neither shall any man pluck them out of my hand. (John 10:28)

> I will never leave thee, nor forsake thee. (Heb. 13:5)

> I am Alpha and Omega, the beginning and the ending, saith the Lord, which is, and which was, and which is to come, the Almighty. (Rev. 1:8)

> The most high God, the possessor of heaven and earth. (Gen. 14:22)

> What man of you having an hundred sheep, if he lost one of them, doth not leave the ninety and nine in the wilderness, and go after that which is lost, until he find it? (Luke 15:4)

Those of us who are faithful must always be encouragers to the world and our fellow brothers and sisters in Christ by reminding them, "The Lord is not slack concerning his promises, as some men count slackness; but is longsuffering to us-ward, not willing that any should perish, but that all should come to repentance" (2 Pet. 3:9).

How do we get our joy back once we allow the enemy to steal it? Restoration is best resolved when starting at the root of the problem. "Be ye transformed by the renewing of your mind" (Rom. 12:2). The word *renew* suggests getting rid of existing thoughts by taking them captive. "Casting down imaginations, and every high thing that exalteth itself against the knowledge of God, and bringing into captivity every thought to the obedience of Christ" (2 Cor. 10:5). In order to take control of the unwanted imaginations, we have to admit that they are there and have a genuine desire to be rid of them. Only then can the healing process begin. It's not enough to try to manage sin; we must acknowledge it and put it behind us. God hates sin. His Son died cruelly on the cross to bring it into captivity. When we recognize just how harmful sin is, we will understand how it separates us from God. Therefore, we must take charge of our circumstances, thoughts, and behaviors. We must reject sin in order to get our joy back.

The mind is a powerful thing. The words we speak on ourselves, whether they are negative or positive, is who we will become. People of the world have their opinions of who they think you are or should be, but God, the Creator of the universe, said, "Ye are a chosen generation, a royal priesthood, an holy nation, a peculiar people; that ye should shew forth the praises of him who hath called you out of darkness into his marvelous light" (1 Pet. 2:9). We must tell ourselves: I am no longer obligated to serve sin (Rom. 6:6), but I am a new creation in Christ (2 Cor. 5:17). I have "redemption through his blood, the forgiveness of sins, according to the riches of his grace" (Eph. 1:7). Therefore, I am free in Christ Jesus (Gal. 5:1) "in whom I also trusted, after that I heard the word of truth, the gospel of my salvation: in whom also after that I believed, I was sealed with the Holy Spirit of promise" (Eph. 1:13). So, I am seated "in heavenly places in Christ Jesus" (Eph. 2:6). Because of who I am, "I press toward the mark for the prize of the high calling of God in Christ Jesus" (Phil. 3:14).

It's high time to stop looking back and press forward. This won't always be easy. Sometimes when we press against the storm, depending upon the force of the wind, it may push us back. The enemy will place furious circumstances in our lives, but we've got superior power on our side. Don't give up—push back. You can read about Moses in Exodus 14:13, when God told him to stand still and see the salvation of the Lord. It's not literally standing still but calming down, telling the people to free their hearts of fear, and watching how God takes them through. In the book of Joshua, God told Joshua to go into battle and take the land of Canaan. In actuality, God was going to fight and win the war; Joshua simply had to go into battle. The key word here is *take*. If you want your joy back, sometimes you have to take it because the enemy doesn't want to let go. He loves seeing you depressed, hurt, angry, defeated, and spiritually down. He has one agenda, and that is to use you for his kingdom work. Be sober (clear-headed) be vigilant (watchful), "because your adversary [enemy] the devil, as a roaring lion, walketh about, seeking [looking for] whom he may devour" (1 Pet. 5:8). Stay focused. It is this evil spirit that is keeping you from living in the joy of the Lord. Getting your joy back is as easy as changing your mind-set from captivity to liberty. The battle is the Lord's. "Be still, and know that I am God" (Ps. 46:10). All you have to do is "call upon the LORD, who is worthy to be praised: so shall I be saved from mine enemies" (Ps. 18:3). Always remember, "without faith it is impossible to please him: for he that cometh to God must believe that he is, and that he is a rewarder of them that diligently seek him" (Heb. 11:6).

Stir up the gift of faith, which is merely an unconditional belief in someone or something. The ultimate assurance of the mind is to believe beyond a shadow of a doubt that Jehovah is God and that he sent Jesus to reconcile humans back to himself by his death on the cross, which gave us the gift of the Holy Ghost when he rose on the third day with all power. This type of faith doesn't come and go with circumstances but remains steadfast in spite of situations or conditions. Let us stir it up to activate the power of God in our lives so that we may persuade others by the evidence demonstrated in us.

It is unbelievably sad to see how so many people are living in defeat. The hopelessness that consumes the minds of so many people is disturbing. It appears that the stronghold of bondage has knocked the legs out from under millions, and they see no hope in getting back up again. Unfortunately, the need to have things, money, popularity, fame, or an extravagant lifestyle keeps too many individuals in bondage. This kind of slavery has inconveniently captured the minds of Christians and has led to depression. How many friends and family do you know who are trapped in a psychosomatic illness? They are simply imprisoned by their own way of thinking and failing to believe that Jesus is the way of escape. Now is the time for the faithful saints of God to reveal faith to those who are broken, torn, or gasping for air. "But they that will be rich fall into temptation and a snare, and into many foolish and hurtful lusts, which drown men in destruction and perdition. For the love of money is the root of all evil: which while some coveted after, they have erred from the faith, and pierced themselves through with many sorrows" (Tim. 6:9). The word *pierced* suggests puncturing or making a hole in something. This hole isn't interpreted as being physical; instead, it insinuates an act against the soul of a person. "Pierced themselves through" means this thing of great force has entered into the soul and is working its way throughout the mind and body. In other words, it is bringing many sorrows that lead to a deep, dark depression.

Our high-mindedness can't help them. Our self-centeredness won't encourage them. Patronizing will only cause them to sink deeper. The only thing that we can give them that will have an effect on their lives is the love of Jesus. We have to see people through spiritual eyes. Observe how we receive counsel from others. We often examine how things are going in their lives before we actually apply their instructions to our own lives. We must be sure that faith is revealed in us before we can enforce it on someone else. If it's not working for you, if it's not real to you, if you are stressed, if you are worried and can't sleep at night, if you don't have a testimony, then you discover where your faith lies before inflicting it on others. "Fight the good fight of faith, lay hold on eternal life, *whereunto thou art also called*, and hast professed a good profession before many witnesses" (1 Tim. 6:12).

Chapter 3

The Sick among Us

When the world looks at Christians, who do they see? Do they see a loving community of people embracing one another, encouraging, and being hospitable, or do they see a bunch of critics and hypocrites? What do they see? Do they see pastors preaching in love and in compassion for people, or to raise money? What do they

> And the prayer of faith shall save the sick, and the Lord shall raise him up; and if he have committed sins, they shall be forgiven him. (James 5:15)

see? Do they see Christians leading by exemplifying Christ, or the "Do as I say, not as I do" mentality? These questions don't apply to the manipulative appearance displayed in the foreground, but the real truth that the world sees lurking in the background.

Christians are called to be a tool of God to lead lost souls to Christ. It is essential that saints never lose focus of the mission. Sinners who are seeking the truth look to God's children for direction. They don't know who Jesus is, where to find him, or how to obtain his knowledge with understanding.

There's a lot being said in James 5:15 about prayer, faith, and being made whole again. The operative word used in this text is *shall*, which suggests certainty. The author James uses euphemisms as he talks to the saints about God with instructions on how to handle the sick in the body of Christ. Reaching out to the world but failing to pray for those in the family is an act of falsifying. The Bible teaches us to put those in the household of faith first because we are of one body. Therefore, trying to impress the world is disappointing to God. This isn't his way of doing things, and neither is it why we have been called. God wants us to show love toward one another first, and then the world can see what love is and what it does. We should start by using the most powerful communicative tool we have: prayer.

Praying for certain people can be difficult at times, or it can be downright hard. So how do we pray for those who make life hard for us? Perhaps we can start by praying for ourselves. It's not always about praying for others, but rather dealing with the grudge or hurt we are holding inside that's not allowing us to pray for them. (Jesus prayed for those who crucified him in his innocence; surely, we can pray for those talking about us.) When seeking a true change of heart, try fasting and prayer for deliverance. Let's not play the blame game, which seems to be the scapegoat for many people out of convenience. Remember, excuses only work for humans, not God. Therefore, it is important to search ourselves by the word of God to be freed of the spiritual bondage that keeps us from praying for others.

Praying should be done in faith. Don't waste precious time saying a daily speech that has no significant meaning. What good is it for us to get on our knees and say empty prayers? It's just you in a room, so who is there to impress? If the prayer isn't real, God's Holy presence isn't there, so what's the purpose? If we take the time to bow our heads, why not make it count? We often say a "nothing prayer" and then tell the person in need of prayer, "I've been praying for you." Prayer is a conversation with God that should not be taken lightly. It is another opportunity to be in his glorious presence. Let us take advantage of this wonderful gift of talking with a Holy God at any given place or time.

When a person is sick, it is often necessary to get medical attention. When a person has grown weary or depressed, it is required that the saints pray. Proverbs 27:17 teaches us that as "Iron sharpeneth iron; so a man sharpeneth the countenance of his friend." We should always encourage and pray for each other and not tear one another down. It's not for the benefit of oneself, but for the edifying of the body, as Paul writes in Ephesians 4:16.

A hospital is a place of trained professionals with the sole purpose of taking care of the sick, attending to other health needs, and providing financial assistance. If the hospital staff is sick, who will treat the patients? The house of prayer is a spiritual hospital, but if the servants are sick, how can the church provide divine spiritual help? Is the local assembly merely a meeting place? Are there people in the body simply doing enough to get by but not holding sincerely to the faith? Every Sunday, the house of God is filled with people singing glorious songs to the Lord, lifting holy hands, and shouting. Meanwhile, inwardly there's hate, unclean thoughts toward others, and backbiting. If this is happening in the house, what's happening to those who don't know the Lord? They are searching for the hope that the church is failing to reveal. The Bible says, "If my people which are called by my name, shall humble themselves, and pray, and seek my face, and turn from their wicked ways" (2 Chron. 7:14). God wouldn't have to mention this in the Bible if it wasn't necessary. It's time for the children of God to stop fighting one another and come together to stand firm in the Lord to defeat the enemy.

God has given us a powerful weapon called prayer, but let us not forget that "without faith it is impossible to please him" (Heb. 11:6). When a child of God has fallen, we are commanded to pray in faith or not to pray at all. This text says, "It is impossible to please God." The word impossible means unbearable or unmanageable in the general glossary, but the Greek dictionary defines it as "can't be done." God is telling his children to pray for one another, and in order for it to count, it must be done

> Now unto him that is able to do exceeding abundantly above all that we ask or think, according to the power that worketh in us. (Eph. 3:20)

in faith. Therefore, praying for self-edification isn't acknowledged by God. Furthermore, impressing humans but disappointing God is a hindrance in the body of Christ. The blind, can't lead the blind, and neither do "sick prayers" bring healing to a dying world. The house of prayer must maintain a working family by being faithful to God and honestly loving him. The body of Christ must activate his genuine love for the true light to shine. There is a saying that practice makes perfect. We are not born with this kind of love, and therefore once we receive it, we must practice, practice, and then practice some more. God will always provide an opportunity to show love toward someone. Some of us receive more opportunities than most because we keep failing the tests. Once we pass the tests, it's time to go to work, allowing each experience to make us more mature. Ask God to give you a heart to love if loving is a challenge for you. God is love, and therefore it is already in you. Seek God! The more we seek and learn of him, the less of ourselves we'll see.

Paul was briefing the Ephesians about their spiritual inheritance. Prior to verse 20 in chapter 3, he was telling them how the Gentiles became a part of the family of God and the spiritual aspects of it. This caused the Ephesians to be a little uneasy about their future, but Paul ended chapter three with powerful encouraging words. Paul gave them information and prayed for them, but he concluded with the authoritative superior power of it all.

The word *now* in this text suggests a new perspective. It removes fear and uncertainty to a more confident mind-set. The standards of God can't ever be reached, and therefore trying to live up to them can be discouraging, but Paul turns the focus unto "Him." Jude says, "Now unto him that is able to keep you from falling" (Jude 1:24). God is all-knowing, all-powerful, and omnipresent, and he can do all things but fail. The Bible says his power works within the saints, which gives us the strength to stand firm. It is this power that allows us to love one another. When we come in contact with those who are hard to love, that's the time to dig deep and look unto him who can do exceedingly, abundantly above all that we ask. What an encouraging truth! No matter what we face, He is more than capable of richly providing beyond what a person could even imagine is enough to take the walk of faith. Christians must understand that Jesus is always available by way of the Holy Spirit to lead us on the path of righteousness for his name's sake. Therefore, our requests for spiritual power have to be within God's ability to perform. He won't or can't respond to unrighteousness; neither can he respond to nonsense. For instance, we can't pray that God punish a person for mistreating us. "For my thoughts are not your thoughts, neither are your ways my ways, saith the LORD" (Isa. 55:8). Operating in love is a requirement. In spite of who the next person is or how that person treats you, God's love has to respond in love. Are there people who will take advantage of your kindness? Yes. Love is the first commandment Jesus gave his people; it also shows a person's position in Christ. "We know that we have passed from death unto life, because we love the brethren" (1 John 3:14).

Knowing how to respond to others in the body of Christ is essential. It helps equip us for witnessing to those who are not familiar with agape. The previous text tells us that God is able to keep us when we are faced with a challenge. It's a matter of staying connected to the power. For example, a refrigerator has the capability of cooling foods at different levels, even to the point of freezing. It maintains fruits, cold-cuts, beverages, dairy, meats, and more. As long as it is connected to the power, it can and will do all that it was designed to do. Christians have a connection to Christ that allows us to witness to people based on their level. Agape is a unique process that can only be managed by the power of God. If we stay connected to the source of our inner power, we can operate in genuine love for all of mankind.

Let's not allow another person's character to change who we are. There are times when people will try to send you through the wringer. How do we handle it without losing composure? Jesus said, "I say unto you, Love your enemies, bless them that curse you, do good to them that hate you, and pray for them which despitefully use you, and persecute you" (Matt. 5:44). God is aware of evildoers because his Son was put through the wringer so that we could be saved. When people are getting on your nerves, don't retaliate or respond negatively. Go to God and tell him, "Lord, John Doe is getting on my nerves. I need you to help me and to intervene to resolve this issue." Be frank and tell him what's on your mind. He knows your thoughts, and therefore, trying to pray in a cute way or hiding your true feelings won't make the situation better. It will actually prolong the petition. For instance, if you are frustrated, an "organized" or " proper" prayer won't flow naturally. You will search for the right words and how to say them, or you'll be repetitious. God wants us to be real and not try to entertain him. Have you ever had people try to explain a situation, but they were talking in circles? Let us be direct with God. "But when ye pray use not vain repetitions, as the heathen do: for they think that they shall be heard for their much speaking" (Matt. 6:7).

The sick among us are suffering from an illness that affects the mind, the body, and the soul (which psychologist call the psyche). Psychology is the study of the mind and of behavior patterns. God created the mind to be intelligent with the ability to multitask. According to the *DK Science Encyclopedia*, the brain is in touch with the body at all times. It contains billions of neurons that link up with each other and with all of the nerves in the body. Scientists know a lot about individual neurons, but the way that the whole brain works is not fully understood. Experts are beginning to discover how we think or remember things. It is known that the brain is divided into separate areas. Some areas deal with the general running of the body. Others are involved in coordinating the movements or in understanding spoken words. The brain is divided into three main regions. Two of them are to look after the functions of the body the brain stem and the cerebellum. They control your breathing, your circulation, and your posture. The cerebrum, which is much larger, processes information. It is this part of the brain that is used to think.

The psyche controls the mental stability of a person. This is why it is never good to say "I know what a person is thinking," or "I know why a person reacted a certain way." The mind is a powerful tool, and no one really knows what a person is thinking. An educated guess is not a fact; it is guess and nothing more. This is why this kind of illness has to be treated by the Maker. It's a spiritual issue that only God can fix.

The Greek word for body is somatic. When God breathed into man's body, it became a living soul. When God calls the soul out of the body, it will become a corpse, which means life no longer exists in it. The body reacts to the conditions of the soul. The soul is full of emotions developing from a person's past that began as young as a toddler for some people. Many marriages fail because the couple is unaware of each other's past prior to the marriage. Therefore, after marriage, the soul began to reveal the hidden emotional secrets, causing lots of problems for one or both partners. A person can only hide the inner self for a period of time. In most cases, something will occur in life to bring those feelings back to the surface unless they are dealt with.

Once a person confesses hope in Christ, the Spirit of God enters into the body, creating a new individual due to the divine presence of the Holy Spirit. The Spirit of God has captured that person for life, but now that the Spirit is present, it begins the healing and purifying process of the soul. The person is saved, but the soul has to start removing those things that are not of God. This is the battle that Christians war against every day. The devil tempts the body with sin, and the Spirit of God is there as the comforter to remove them. This illness that's running havoc in the body of Christ is called psychosomatic illness. The mind, body, and soul are disagreeing and thus causing confusion within the inner self. People react to psychosomatic illnesses in different ways. Therefore, when people gossip all the time, it's a spiritual sickness. To see people full of hate is a sign that they are still dealing with a psychosomatic illness. The same illness is keeping those who compulsively lie, cheat, steal, curse, or kill. The cure isn't talking about them. Jesus came to teach us how to love the unlovable and reach the unreachable. There's power in his name, and we can reach him through prayer. This is the hard part, but it is the most important part. Let us deny self so that God can use us in our lifestyle, witness, and prayers to save the sick who are among us.

Chapter 4

We Have Guests

W e always make sure the house is clean whenever guests are expected. Even if the guests are family, a big spring cleaning can be anticipated. Why? Some people might say they clean to impress their guests; for others, it's the only time the house gets

> Saints are witnesses to the world that Jesus is alive; therefore, the inner man must be clean to be affective.

cleaned. A few do it to make their guests comfortable, and someone else might clean house because it's expected.

The temple of God and a brick-and-mortar structure requires cleaning for different reasons. One building is designed to house an invisible guest, and the other building is designed to house visible ones. Spiritual cleaning is done to replicate divine living.

Saints need to clean thoroughly every day with the word of God in preparation for daily living. Sinners don't know how to conduct themselves or how to dress in God's house. We have to clean up to be the example. Home training teaches children how to act, whether at home, at school, at a store, or visiting others. Church training is essential for babes in Christ, especially when there are visitors who may enter in the house of prayer.

Idle gossip that goes on in the church is spiritually life-threatening to tender young souls. James 3:8 tells us that "the tongue is an unruly evil, full of deadly poison." Talking out of pride or malice interferes with truth and learning God's peace. We should speak only of whatsoever things are true, honest, just, pure, lovely, and of a good report, as Paul writes in Philippians. Too often gossip is welcomed among the children of God. It has become quite common for parents to slander others in the presence of their own children, thus teaching them the skill so they may carry it on to the next generation. Teaching is teaching, whether it is good or bad. The Greek word *Diábolos* can be translated as slanderer or devil. A Christian's character shouldn't be identified with Satan, but this great evil of badmouthing others is practiced routinely in the house of prayer. Unfortunately, many may claim to be Christians but fail to live the absolute truth before their children. God is still waiting for those who are called by his name.

Adultery in the church places a handicap on the body. Why a handicap? This sin (and others) is present among the leaders of God's house. Ungodliness practiced among the members is a hindrance to the body, but those who are leading by example (so to speak) are in a position to bring even more harm to God's people, and to those who don't know him. This type of behavior causes spiritual setbacks, and God is not pleased.

Jealousy in the church sends out negative tension, which prevents the Spirit of God from moving freely in his house. Power and positions in the church have taken hold of people, who have forgotten that service is to the glorification of God and not themselves. Working in the local assembly is a duty to God. It is ungodly to take on a position but fail to follow through because we can't work in a shared position with a friend. Moreover, leaving a church because we no longer hold a wanted position is selfish. God will not reward or honor work done in his house for the primary purpose of making money. Many preachers are tricked by Satan and fall into this category. Running after money but failing to have a heart for saving souls leads to many evils in the house of prayer. In one case, a young preacher was spiritually

> And above all things have fervent charity among yourselves: for charity shall cover the multitude of sins. Use hospitality one to another without grudging. (1 Pet. 8–9)

damaged because he was influenced by preachers who follow their greed. After twenty-plus years as a minister of the gospel, he still has a heart for God, but his main focus has turned to exposing corrupt preachers to help people see the man in the pulpit as he truly is. (Is he a man for God or a man for the dollar?) God is still waiting for those who are called by his name.

Many sins are lurking in God's house, but for a Christian (those called by God's name) to live willfully under the command of these sins brings shame to the name of God. We say we're his, but we live as though we aren't. This makes us bad hosts to our guests and bad ambassadors for Christ. "Walk in the Spirit, and ye shall not fulfill the lust of the flesh" (Gal. 5:16).

The Bible teaches us that we all fall short of God's glory; therefore, none of us can point fingers at another. Instead, we must show love in order to mimic Christ. Let's not dwell in sin, but let's pray for one another's deliverance so that we may live in harmony. A song that is sung in harmony makes a good and pleasant sound, but one instrument or one voice that is off-key makes a noticeable noise.

The world is full of people hurting for one reason or another. Those who struggle are plenteous: drug and alcohol addicts, pedophiles, prostitutes, and adulterers; victims of human trafficking, of rape, sexual molestation, and incest; physical abusers, battered women and children; serial killers, mass murderers, and suicides; money launderers, thieves, unethical politicians, gamblers/coveters/lovers of money; and many others. Many of these people are struggling to be free, but they don't know how to liberate themselves. Seeing people hurting continuously and going through so much, even to the point of living in fear, is painful. This troubles us.

How does God feel about those of us who say we know him yet fail to reveal him to a dying world? We know that he is self-existent, all-knowing, infinite, and unfailingly powerful, present in time and eternity all at once. We know that we can call on the name of Jesus to make pain, sickness, addictions, fears, and anything of darkness flee. The world doesn't know all this. We must stop carrying on about our petty differences and start living for Christ. The world needs us to be real and stop making everything about us. She bought a dress like yours. So what? He sings better. So what? You don't like the way I wear my hair. So what? Our lives aren't about that. So what? He can memorize more scripture. So what? That church has more members. The world is dying, and we as the body of Christ is fighting among ourselves, making ourselves unavailable for God's purpose. He made us and saved us, so we belong to him. Let's get over ourselves so that we can help people who are searching for the truth. Saints get on a soapbox about their pastor doing too much, the church being too big, the kind of ministries they have, and how another church is operating. Stay focused. In Matthew 4, Satan tempted Jesus three times. The first time, he came to Jesus to tempt him, but the second time, he took Jesus to the top of the temple, and the last time, he took him to a high mountain. Glory to God, Jesus didn't come for the things of this world. He was on a mission: to give us "the ministry of reconciliation" (2 Cor. 5:18). He didn't allow the devil to distract him from his purpose. The Bible teaches us to resist the devil, and he will flee. The word *will* suggest certainty, so we won't have to second-guess our actions. "God is not a man that he should lie" (Num. 23:19). Thus, he is still waiting for those who are called by his name to humble ourselves, seek his face, and turn from our wicked ways so that healing can take place.

Chapter 5

Working for the Lord

The job market consists of many professions with skilled people capable of performing well in each field. Some people are naturally talented to complete any task in their specialty, whether they are laborers, technicians, engineers, nurses, doctors, public relations professionals, lawyers, or teachers. God can use everyone's talents for witnessing to others. Those working in communications are great assets to the kingdom of God because they speak to thousands of people each day. Secular careers and careers in the ministry are often viewed in a different light. But God can use any job or position for his purpose. Christians should apply God's standards while performing secular jobs such as a secretary, company president, lawyer, custodian, teacher, and so on. Service in the world is still witnessing, as if we were operating within the church. "Servants, obey in all things your masters according to the flesh; not with eyeservice, as menpleasers; but in singleness of heart, fearing God: And whatsoever ye do, do it heartily, as to the Lord, and not unto men" (Col. 3:22–23). Working for a boss "as to the Lord" doesn't mean making our employers gods, but rather doing the task that has been set before us by those in authority over us. Although it is certain that managers and supervisors are sometimes power-driven, which can make jobs difficult, Christians must remain faithful in our choice to be children of God. Certainly, we are often

> For we are his workmanship, created in Christ Jesus unto good works, which God hath before ordained that we should walk in them. (Eph. 2:10)

mistreated by biased management or taken advantage of because of our willingness to do what's right. Thus, working "as unto the Lord" isn't always easy because it means we must endure difficult tests. "For thy sake we are killed all the day long" (Rom. 8:36). In other words, we take up the daily cross of suffering and follow him (Luke 9:23). This suffering also applies to the work place. Wherever God has positioned us to witness, we must stay focused on our mission. We should get revived in the house of God by his word, so that our hearts will be ready to take on the world.

We will always find an opportune time in the church to practice working "as unto the Lord." Those who hold positions in the church operate under a sense of ownership instead of worship. But everything that we do is to the glory of God. Even when faced with oppositions, we have an opportunity to let God shine through us. The positions we hold are God using us to carry out his will. Promotions in secular jobs also afford opportunities to serve others at a higher level. Receiving advancement is exciting, but after the happiness wears off, let's ask God how that position can be used to serve him. Perhaps we can affect colleagues who have never been to church, or we can touch a community of people who are within our reach for the first time. Or possibly our financial reward can help someone we've always wanted to help but couldn't previously afford to.

Let's not forget that we are on a journey for Christ even when it comes to money. For example, your mother sent you to the store with twenty dollars to make a purchase. Along the way, you faced several distractions, but you knew what would happen if you weren't home on time. You make this journey with one mission in mind: getting to the store, making the purchase, and getting back home on time. The thing is your mother didn't tell you how much time you had; she simply said to hurry back. On your way back home, you helped a lady with her bags, helped someone across the street, threw a kid's ball back in the yard after it rolled into the street, and did a few other things. When you got home, your mother said, "You got home sooner than I anticipated. Good job, son."

This story basically describes our Christian journey. We're on a trip for Jesus, working until he calls us home. He provides our spiritual and material needs. He simply asks for 10 percent toward keeping and building his kingdom, and for us to give a portion to help those less fortunate. He tells us to avoid unnecessary distractions and stay focused on our calling. Every time we go on a trip, it's about Jesus, not about us. When we agree to work for a ministry in the church or to go on mission trips, it is an arrangement with God, not humans. When we fail to do what we agreed to do, we're breaking a promise to God because this is his kingdom. It is crucial that we stop making the spiritual walk about us.

"For do I now persuade men, or God? Or do I seek to please men? for if I yet pleased men, I should not be the servant of Christ" (Gal. 1:10). Service is not meant to praise men. Failing to work for the right motives only reflects your relationship with Christ. The next person knowing how well we performed is meaningless, especially if our work is merely for recognition. How can a person serve God and humankind when their standards are not the same? We find a word of wisdom in the voice of truth written in the book of Acts by Luke: "We ought to obey God rather than men." We experience a sense of satisfaction within when a service is performed. The joy of the Lord fills our hearts, knowing that he is pleased. This kind of joy doesn't come from people pleasing. People are constantly changing their minds and having different opinions, but God never changes. He is the same yesterday, today, and forever. So, let us be mindful of who we are in Christ and live for his purpose. The scriptures tell us that we are bought with a price; we are not our own.

We are working in the kingdom of God as a result of being saved. This makes us the servants of Christ. If we choose to please men instead of God, we are idle in our service. Not allowing God's temple to be used for his purpose is a form of spiritual sickness for which a spiritual doctor is needed for treatment. "If man therefore purge himself from these he shall be a vessel unto honour, sanctified, and meet [fit] for the master's use, and prepared unto every good work" (2 Tim. 2:21).

Chapter 6

The Analyst

The devil has a problem with saints and whom they represent, so don't be surprised when people come against us without cause or without proof of their accusations. Using God's people against each other is his specialty. All he needs is someone who talks a lot and someone who has an open ear to hearsay to spread rumors. Unfortunately, the local assembly is like a shopping mall: he can find someone of any age, size, or color. But unlike in the mall, people are willing to cut down others for free, with no remorse or concern about destroying a person's reputation.

People who like to analyze the lives of others don't always operate on facts. For them, it's easy to develop and reach a conclusion even when there's no foundation for it. Sadly, some people who claim to be children of God will often listen to rumors and contribute to the lies. Satan will always make gossip convenient. The question is, are we strong enough to resist him? "Out of the same mouth proceedeth blessing and cursing. My brethren, these things ought not so to be" (James 3:10). A popular response to selfishly justify this kind of behavior is, "If it's the truth, it's not gossip, just stating the facts." God is love, and Jesus is the Prince of Peace according to scripture; therefore, he is incapable of permitting or breaking peace of any kind. Jesus said, "If thy brother shall trespass [sin] against thee, go and tell him his fault between thee and him alone" (Matt. 18:15). *Alone* in this text suggests being solo or unaccompanied.

God is against confusion and mess in his house. But cliques and messy people exist throughout the church, working together against poor souls who are trying to serve God in peace to mend this evil world we live in. Why are so many people struggling to work in peace in the church? It's God's house. We are supposed to bring Christ to the house of prayer with us. What's happening to the family of God?

Biblical text makes it clear that all have sinned, which tells us that we will err. He has given instructions on how to handle it: Forgive others as Christ has forgiven us. He isn't telling his children to go around lying to people or broadcasting their personal business in the street. Many times, some Christians may build themselves up by tearing down someone else, and God is not pleased. Our standards are based on the word of God, not humans. Hurting someone's reputation out of selfishness, anger, or a need to impress worldly minds or to make friends is cruel. "Let your moderation be known unto all men. The Lord is at hand" (Phil. 4:5).

The way we treat others should represent Christ, but if we're busybodies, Satan gets the credit, not Christ. Why do we think that we can live deceitful lives, yet God receives our praises during worship service? Do we really believe that God is pleased with us? Are we so sick that we can't see the illness anymore? How can we see the world's spiritual needs when we are blind ourselves? Something has to change within us. The Apostle Paul tells us in 2 Timothy to "stir up the gift of God." He is that same God who did miraculous things for others, and he is more than capable of doing the same things for us today.

Just think for a minute. God is loving, compassionate, caring, and divinely mindful of us. He is incapable of lying, breaking peace, being hateful, or performing any evil deed. Yet those of us who say we're children of God praise him when it's convenient but fail to show love toward our brothers and sisters in Christ. Picking and choosing who to love is merely an imitation of love.

Some will curse their own children, let alone another member of the church. Perhaps God is still waiting for his people who are called by his name. "Looking unto Jesus the author and finisher of our faith; who for the joy that was set before him endured the cross, despising the shame, and is set down at the right hand of the throne of God" (Heb. 12:2). God gave his only son out of love for us. But we are such a selfish people, so much so that we are willfully repaying him for his marvelous works in disobedience. Are we so stubborn that when God says stop, we go? When he says leave, we stay? If he commands us to love, why do we hate? Why can't we love each other the way he has shown love for us?

Words are powerful. Once a word is spoken, it can't be retrieved. So, do we speak words of encouragement or words to tear down? Do we speak words of selfishness or words to honor others? Words of destruction can ruin a person, often for a lifetime. "If any man among you seem to be religious, and bridleth not his tongue, but deceiveth his own heart, this man's religion is vain" (James 1:26). Many may not know this, but God cannot answer prayers that aren't pure. Purposely living a rebellious life with expectations of God's gifts outside of common blessings reveals total ignorance of who God is. It also uncovers a person's true relationship with Christ.

A spirit of negativity has consumed the minds of many people. This spirit has so overtaken them until they can no longer see it. Such a lack of enthusiasm finds fault in everything and everybody. Even good appears bad in their eyes. In God's house, this spirit works through Christians to tear down, prevent action, or cause confusion. Let us be mindful of them, but first let's look at ourselves to be certain that this spirit isn't influencing us too.

We should always start with the self before confronting others. Health is a perfect example of how people fail to view change from a positive perspective. Often when we question people about their health, their responses are so negative one might believe they are already in the grave. Those of us who are stronger in our faith must cut off this conversation and strive to redirect it. Let's find words to lift people up when they begin talking down about themselves. Sometimes what they say is a matter of their pessimistic expectancy. They may have been sick for so long that their bodies are tired. Let us be cautious and not falsely accuse anyone of excessive negativity, because the instigator may very well be the one in the mirror. Let our voices be someone else's sweet song for the day and bring words of joy, peace, and hope to overshadow that destructive spirit.

The gift of being spiritually discerning allows saints of God to see good from evil, according to Hebrews 4:12. Not everyone has this gift, but the word of God gives all saints the knowledge to recognize righteousness from unrighteousness. Christians are not called to be analysts of other people. Saints are merely vessels to be used by God for his glorification alone.

Saints have enough to do with daily Bible study to keep from falling. We don't have time to search the hearts and deeds of others, because by the time God finishes searching us, we'll have plenty of personal errors to mend with God. Let's stop being so judgmental and focus on improving ourselves so that God can use us.

Chapter 7

More Is Required

G od knew before the world began that humans would sin in the garden of Eden. He had a plan in place to work through his reconciled people and help save lost souls. God expects nothing of a sinner due to a lack of knowledge, a lack of power to follow through, and a lack of relationship. A sinner's spiritual state is known as spiritual blindness, which is a mental

> Then they said to him, "What must we do, to be doing the works of God?" Jesus answered them, "This is the work of God, that you believe in him whom he has sent." (John 6:28–29)

state called spiritual darkness. This makes it impossible for God to connect with these people as servants.

Evil caused Adam to sin, which brought about spiritual darkness that still exists today. "Then spake Jesus again unto them, saying, I am the light of the world: he that followeth me shall not walk in darkness, but shall have the light of life" (John 8:12). "Ye are the light of the world" (Matt. 5:14). Christians are the lanterns whom his light shines through. A saint's way of life should give the world hope. It should attract an unsaved person like a magnet; God is expecting nothing less from his children. "Ye are the salt of the earth: but if the salt have lost his savour, wherewith shall it be salted? It is thenceforth good for nothing" (Matt. 5:13). Have you ever had an experience where a crowd of people saw something wondrous? What was their response? "Ooh, aah, wow!" They were overwhelmed with amazement. The lifestyle of saints should have sinners oohing and wowing all day, saying, "I want what they have," as in Acts 16:30: "what must I do to be saved?"

The English dictionary defines hope as an individual's wish for or anticipation of something that may or may not happen. Biblically, it is the absolute expectation of salvation. Hope in Christ is knowing the final destination of the saints. "Looking for that blessed hope, and the glorious appearing of the great God and our Saviour Jesus Christ" (Titus 2:13). Christians should walk in confidence because we know the truth and can show the world how to stand on a word that can't fail. Saints are living on a promise made by God who is incapable of lying. In that assurance, let us reveal the hope of Christ for the entire world to see instead of keeping it so neatly tucked away.

The paparazzi spend their days tracking down celebrities to reveal their images, income, families, and careers to the world. The paparazzi put it all out there. The children of God are the paparazzi for Christ—perhaps not as aggressive, but similarly tasked with plastering Jesus's image everywhere we go. We do this by not withholding our income from those less fortunate, putting family first, and using our careers as tools to witness to others.

Although it is for certain that all jobs won't allow Jesus's name to be exalted, our lifestyles can say plenty without verbally speaking a word. We may or may not be celebrities, but the only true superstar is Jesus Christ. Learning to become more like him should be the ultimate goal for our lives. It's this type of makeover the world needs to see to make a difference. Transformation is the miraculous change that comes over a person once he or she accepts hope in Jesus Christ. In Isaiah 43:2, God reminds Israel that they are his, and as they go through the refinery, he'll be there to carry them through it. The children of God must experience spiritual refinement to become the chaste virgin to Christ mentioned in 2 Corinthians 11:2. The purpose of a refinery is to remove all impurities. He is molding us every day so that when he looks at us, he'll see more of himself.

Jesus place of birth illustrates that even the least can receive salvation. Salvation is not merely for a particular person or a certain group of people, but for all of mankind. He grew up and went about doing his Father's business. I've never read that people were attracted to his possessions, alluring charisma, or his six-figure job. People were simply taken by his characteristics and the things he did. The spiritual refinery shapes us to his image, the inner self shining so brightly that it over shadows the physical self. Let's understand that when we pray and ask God to use us, we should be prepared to go through the purifying process. This method is by God's will and not ours. Therefore, we must go through tests and trials for the purpose of making us stronger to equip us for the battlefield.

Let's not run from God when he answers our prayers. Instead, let's stand patiently during this growing process. Divine preparation is a part of the promise, as Hebrews 6:18–19 implies. A welder can't work without a drill bit. A chef can't cook without food. A football team can't play without the ball, A Christian can't serve without being spiritually equipped. Christianity is a mission for all of us who believe that Jesus is the Son of Jehovah. To be his servant requires living a certain lifestyle, teaching or spreading the gospel, and doing missionary work. But we can't teach what we don't know, and

> For we are saved by hope: but hope that is seen is not hope: for what a man seeth, why doth he yet hope for? But if we hope for that we see not, then do we with patience wait for it. (Rom. 8:24–25)

neither can we give what we don't have. Let us always remember that Christianity is a growing process, and as long as there is life within our bodies, we can thrive in the kingdom of God. Let's not be discouraged by those who may be a little more mature in their spiritual walk. Allowing God to use us where we are will increase spiritual growth. This is one reason why saints are not defined by financial or social status.

Chapter 8

The Mirror

In Corinthians, Paul deals with hidden or public sins that people fail to acknowledge. God gives a fair warning that if Christians fail to search themselves, he will. Consequences are attached to sin

> Examine yourselves, whether ye be in the faith; prove your own selves (2 Cor. 13:5) For if we judge ourselves, we should not be judged. (1 Cor. 11:31)

just as a mirror has a reflection, the sun shines, fire produces heat, or a tornado is accompanied by wind. These things don't exist without their pairs, and sin cannot occur without consequences.

Let's stop making excuses to sin. Let's admit that sin is a problem. Instead of blinding ourselves to reality, we must face it head-on. We must stop allowing the devil to blind us in certain areas of our lives. Playing the ignorance game won't work with God at the judgment. Failing to learn God's word to become better servants won't go over well with him. This can result in receiving fewer rewards.

Refusing to recognize a fault sends a mixed message to the world. Non-believers have no reason to change if Christians are living the same lifestyle as they are. Why should they change? In their perception, Christians live under restrictions, in bondage to this church thing, studying the Bible, and yet they participate in the same sinful activities. Some Christians make following Christ appear burdensome instead of the delightful pleasure that it is. The sinner can't find a reason to accept Jesus when Christians won't face their own weaknesses. We can make a difference in this world because God's word still stands. "If my people, which are called by my name, shall humble themselves, and pray, and shall seek my face, and turn from their wicked ways; *then* will I hear from heaven, and will forgive their sin, and will heal their land" (2 Chron. 7:14).

Unfortunately, this is part of the world's problem. America was founded on the Lord Jesus, but now she has allowed other denominations to eliminate him from nearly everything. God hasn't changed, but the laws of the United States have. According to God, marriage is still between one man and one woman, but the enemy has altered it in the eyes of humans.

God says no other name is greater than that of his Son, Jesus. But the enemy has removed his name from some public places to prevent offending those who have rejected him. If you have guests in your home for several days, and after three days they begin telling you what they don't like and the changes they want to make, what would be your response? It might be something like this: "This is my house. If you don't like it, you can leave."

Why would America allow people from other countries to come into its territory and change the things that matter most? Some people feel that President Obama's stand on being the president for everyone in America and not just Christians can be understood. The problem is that the country's laws are too flexible, which places America in a critical position. For that reason, Christians should continue being faithful servants. "Therefore, my beloved brethren, be ye stedfast, unmoveable, always abounding in the work of the Lord, forasmuch as ye know that your labour is not in vain in the Lord" (1 Cor. 15:58).

Christians should not support ungodly laws. Condoning same-sex marriage, gambling, abortions, and "safe sex" practices as embraced by unbelievers or those who are ignorant of the gospel will setup these United States for persecution. It's understood that a new babe in Christ won't have the biblical knowledge to abstain immediately from sin or have the wisdom to see certain issues from a spiritual perspective. Therefore, Bible study, Sunday school, or some form of biblical learning is crucial for spiritual growth. To be ignorant of God's word only makes one's service ineffective. The Bible also works as a mirror to help reveal the inner self. This is a wakeup call for the saints. Let's get busy for God.

Take this test. Stand before the mirror and ask yourself, "What's in my life that is keeping me from being all that God has called me to be?" It's just you and the mirror, with no one to impress or mislead. Have an open mind and a willing spirit to deal with whatever is there. Allow God to take you through the purifying process to get rid of your weaknesses. If you've done this and have no sin in your life, go to your secret place, where it's just you and the Lord, and pray, "Search me, O God, and know my heart: try me, and know my thoughts: And see if there be any wicked way in me, and lead me in the way everlasting" (Ps. 139:23–24). Maybe you've taken the test but can only see the faults of others. Perhaps these are people you deal with on a daily basis, and you really need them to change. You might want to ask God for spiritual insight, which is vital for your soul. Instead of praying about a friend's faults, consult with God to address the issues of the one you see in the mirror. The Bible is God's unique way of advising how to live and how to be in control of one's own life. It reflects the life of Jesus so that we will know who we are and whose we are. Readers should individually reflect on the Bible because it consists of personal letters from God to you. "For if any be a hearer of the word, and not a doer, he is like unto a man beholding his natural face in a glass: For he beholdeth himself, and goeth his way, and straightway forgetteth what manner of man he was" (James 1:23–24). How can a person walk away from the mirror without washing off bread crumbs, smeared makeup, and toothpaste? Once the Bible makes known a person's flaws, why would anyone close the book or place the blame on someone else?

We can't lead others to Christ when we can't admit to our own sins. Releasing pressure in a time of anger might seem justifiable. Some people know what buttons to push in order to pull you away from your purpose-driven life. Although expressing yourself or perhaps giving them a piece of your mind may appear reasonable, God says this behavior doesn't encourage holiness. "Why beholdest thou the mote [speck] that is in thy brother's eye, but considerest not the beam that is in thine own eye?" (Matt. 7:3).

"For the wrath of man worketh not the righteousness of God" (James 1:20). Our angry dispositions aren't permissible to God simply because the physical over takes the spiritual. Think of the consequences of speaking impulsively. It's unmistakably clear that your words may make you feel good, but how does it affect the other person? Is your approach a positive or a negative one? Does it make things better or worse? Most important, how does God see it?

Sleepwalkers involuntarily function senselessly. If God isn't pleased, the situation is still unresolved. The discrepancy is even more crucial now because we have a person who is spiritually asleep and a Christian operating as though he's sleeping. So where is the solution? Sleepwalkers involuntarily function senselessly. Surely those of us who are awake can function better than someone who isn't operating consciously.

The blind leading the blind will result in two people falling in the ditch. We can't respond to matters as those who are of the world or as those who have fallen asleep. Take a look in the mirror and tell God what you see. He already knows what's there, but he can't help us until we face our faults and run to Jesus in repentance. "As many as I love, I rebuke and chasten: be zealous therefore, and repent" (Rev. 3:19).

Chapter 9

It's Not Okay

The Bible teaches that ambassadors for Christ are examples for the world. Compromising God's word only functions as a hindrance for people who are ignorant of the truth. It is vital that Christians don't perform or respond to situations in the same fashion as the world. Helping the sin-sick souls, reaching out to those broken, being a shoulder for the weak, and lending a helping hand to those less fortunate requires that the Spirit of God work in full force within the saints. The flesh is sinful, and so it should not be the basis for decision making. Why? "That which is born of the flesh is flesh; and that which is born of the Spirit is spirit" (John 3:6).

Jesus is clear in his sayings. Unfortunately, some people believe they are justified in their choices to operate outside of God's will. They forget who they are in Christ and act as irrational individuals. For instance, it's not okay to wish harm toward any individuals. To speak negatively about someone isn't okay, regardless of the circumstances. Cheering when someone fails at something because you were mistreated isn't okay. God is not okay with sinful mind-sets, no matter how we may defend our actions. God is only concerned about those things encouraged by the Holy Spirit.

> Vengeance is mine; I will repay, saith the Lord. (Rom. 12:19)

> Judge not. (John 7:1)

Blessed is the man that walketh not in the counsel of the ungodly, nor standeth in the way of sinners, nor sitteth in the seat of the scornful. (Ps. 1:1)

Repent: for the kingdom of heaven is at hand. (Matt. 4:17)

For this (love sake) Thou shalt not commit adultery, Thou shalt not kill, Thou shalt not steal, Thou shalt not bear false witness, Thou shalt not covet; and if there be any other commandment, it is briefly comprehended in this saying, namely, Thou shalt love thy neighbor as thyself. (Rom. 13:9)

Children are often told by siblings or sometimes parents, "Didn't I tell you not to get up there? That's why you fell. Maybe you'll listen next time." Perhaps adults respond negatively to others with words such as "He was so ugly to me. I hope he gets what he deserves." Or "She's always talking about people. I wonder how she feels now that it's happening to her. I'm glad it happened."

How pure are our thoughts toward others or the way we respond to one another? Christians ought not to think like this. "For as he thinketh in his heart, so is he" (Prov. 23:7). Christians frequently find fault in others, but the problem really lies within the accuser. Thinking impure thoughts toward others is a sure sign that self-assessment is needed. Let's not play the blame game. Rather, let's seek God for spiritual deliverance so that he can work through us, instead of us working against him.

It's disturbing how Christians can encourage and speak immoral things toward others—sometimes in the same breath—and then immediately try to justify it, as if that will make it right with God. It's not okay to be hateful. It's not okay to accuse others falsely. It's not okay to react to rumors. It is certainly not okay to retaliate, not even within your imagination.

Chapter 10

The Heart of a Child

Families were God's unique idea from the beginning. There's no better place to learn the essential principles of life than within the family. Nowhere can the truths of God's word be more effectively taught and modeled than in the home. On the contrary, there is no institution or group of people who has more power and ability to destroy a person than the family. Physical and verbal abuse, as well as neglect, selfish motives, and illicit behaviors, can damage the emotional well-being of a child well into adulthood, and often for a lifetime (Beers, 1996).

The failure of parents to teach spiritual truths to their children directly impacts their children's relationship with God and how they treat others. Family is the environment that shapes a child's lifetime direction. Differences in personalities and characteristics make it evident that all children won't respond to parental instructions or embrace their training in the same manner. Therefore, it is crucial for Christians to seek God's guidance for handling each child based on individuality.

Parenting is more than teaching, giving instructions, and taking disciplinary actions. Parenting is showing a child how to live and love by being an example. Discussing a matter instead of yelling about it can be a great nurturing tool. Perhaps being truthful in speech and actions can be an even better form of child rearing than simply telling children what they must do.

Children can easily receive mixed signals when parents act one way at home but behave differently in public. Why should they believe they're loved when parents aren't behaviorally consistent? Being dishonest in our conduct is the same as lying with words; therefore, when we lie to our children, we give them reason to be doubtful of storge. Storge is a Greek word for love, meaning the natural affection a parent has for a child.

How should parents handle a rebellious child who is receiving genuine love and affection? In some cases, a child may have his or her own idea of what love is, which makes meeting the child's needs very difficult for the parents. No matter how affectionate the parents are, the child isn't getting it. Their mixed communication is causing a problem, leaving the parents anxious and the child feeling unloved. Children can then find themselves looking for the wrong kind of love in the wrong places, and they can fall into all sorts of evils. Peers may also be cruel in making fun of other children, whether at school, on social media, or at social events, deeply affecting a teased or bullied child.

Children being allowed to come and go as they please, or to do whatever they want, gives them a misperception of love. But another child might see it as real love and begin thinking he or she was born into the wrong family. Yet another child who is being molested can't see love as a reality. Perhaps one loving parent doesn't know the child is suffering. Maybe both parents are nurturing, but an uncle, aunt, sister, or brother is causing the child to feel unloved. Still another child lives in a home where the parents favor one child over the other, causing the less favored child to feel unwanted.

Many situations and household conditions can cause children to feel as if no one loves them. Trauma or abuse can place them into a mental prison even when they have loving and trustworthy people in their lives. So, how can we convince children to see that they are loved when it seems impossible for them? "Suffer little children to come unto me, and forbid them not, for of such is the kingdom of heaven" (Luke 18:16). We might think they are too young to understand.

The Bible says the disciples thought the children were bothering Jesus, but Jesus says, "Bring the little children to me." We can do several things for our children to be acquainted with love. We start by teaching them biblical text to lead them to Christ. The more they learn, the more their curiosity arises. This process builds a foundation that will one day allow them to hear the holy call. Helping our children find their way back home is our primary goal. This process will also teach them how to cope with life's issues and find the one thing they've been longing for: true love, which is in Jesus Christ. We should faithfully take them to God in prayer, the most powerful and the most important tool we have. "Whatsoever ye shall ask in prayer, believing, ye shall receive" (Matt. 21:22).

Getting involved is another way to reveal love to them and draw them closer. They may not always consult a parent, even if the relationship is close. But it's okay for them to confide in another trustworthy adult, someone who can help them see agape. The key is getting them to open up, instead of keeping those harmful feelings and thoughts trapped inside. Did you know Satan put those thoughts in their minds, affecting their emotions, which could lead to dreadful endings? This is his goal.

But we saints of God are going to put a stop to it! We are going to stop pretending we're listening and take the time to actually hear what the children have to say. This doesn't necessarily mean hearing what's coming out of their mouths, but hearing what they are saying by their actions. Some of our children are screaming for attention from Mom and Dad. We're going to stop putting work and friends before their needs and even some of their wants. We're going to support our children by helping with homework, and when we can't help, we'll find someone who can. We'll support them in extracurricular activities. We're going to take our children back by fighting using something that never fails: love! What about when they are being hard-headed? When they test us, we'll be firm with love. Think about it: they aren't smarter than we are. We've all been children, so if we pay close attention to them, we can always be one step ahead. I know we can do this if we stop being too busy for our children and do what God is asking of his children. Awaken and stir up the gift of Jesus.

Chapter 11

Never Forget Our Purpose

It is apparent that the modus operandi for many of today's Christians is so deeply engulfed in self-satisfaction that we refuse to be inconvenienced. Notice how certain people are looked down upon by churchgoers, who are failing to fellowship with them. Examine how church people make excuses for not giving of themselves because it interferes with their daily schedules. Look at how church is the first thing to be eliminated when the schedule becomes overloaded.

Conversely, a handful of people are willing to be worn out for the Lord. Being on the battlefield for the Lord isn't a game for this faithful minority; it's working in the church with hopes of waking up a few who are asleep. Those sleeping don't realize they have work to do. The sin in their lives has awakened, thus putting them to sleep. If the faithful minority will continue in faithfulness, the power of God will move to awaken their fellow Christians and return sin to its sleep.

Working on the battlefield for the Lord isn't simply helping those we choose, but who God says is in need. The battlefield doesn't necessarily mean we'll be working in a nursing home or a shelter. It could very well mean serving in our own homes. Learning at church (the classroom) is great, but sometimes God takes us on a field trip for hands-on assignments. Let's not get caught up in trying to do something extravagant for the entire world to see, when some of us can actually do our greatest work with our own family members.

For instance, we ask God to use us in the parents' ministry, youth ministry, the singles' ministry, or the couples' ministry, but serving is serving no matter where the need is. Helping our own children deal with problems is no different from helping someone else's child. Let us not forget that God sees souls, not flesh. Whether there's a confused soul in your home or a confused person in the next person's home needing guidance and prayer, God will use us wherever he sees the need.

Never forget that we didn't call ourselves to salvation; it's by the grace of God. Never forget that we can't keep ourselves; it is the power of God that maintains us. Never forget that we are saved for a purpose, and this purpose includes witnessing to our fellow brothers and sisters in Christ. Never forget "there is no respecter of persons with God" (Rom. 2:11); therefore, we should not be bias. Never forget that we are held accountable for our service as Christians. Never forget that Jesus "hath saved us, and called us with an holy calling, not according to our works, but according to his own purpose and grace, which was given us in Christ Jesus before the world began" (2 Tim. 1:9). Never forget that it's not about us. Never forget our purpose: the Great Commission (Matt. 28:16).

A mission such as this requires the unique ability to have godly love (Gal. 5:22–23). In the book of Romans, Paul teaches Christians how to respond to issues directly related to people in the family of God: if prophecy, let us prophesy in proportion to our faith; or ministry, let us use it in our ministering; he who teaches, in teaching; he who exhorts, in exhortation; he who gives, with liberality; he who leads, with diligence; he who shows mercy, with cheerfulness. The twelfth chapter of Romans goes into details as to how saints should treat one another. He advises Christians to love without hypocrisy, to hate things of evil, and to cling to that which is good. He encourages saints to be leaders and show others the way by treating each other affectionately with brotherly love.

Many times we get lazy, but according to scripture we should be on fire for the Lord. "Rejoicing in hope; patient in tribulation; and continuing instant in prayer" (Rom. 12:12). We should also express the spirit of sharing, even when we are mistreated or cursed. It isn't easy to be faithful at all times, but we should rejoice with them who do rejoice, and weep with them who weep, even when we don't feel up to it. Let us "be of the same mind one toward another" (Rom. 12:16), not thinking too highly of ourselves or failing to meet people at their levels, especially when witnessing. Too many Christians fall short in this area because they want to categorize sin and place judgment on others based on their own levels of spiritual growth. Fortunately, God doesn't hold his maturity level against the unlearned Christian. He is well aware that godliness doesn't come overnight, so we must be patient with those just starting out, just as God is patient with us.

When a child is being potty trained, repeated teaching is required. Mom knows that she'll have to tell her child the same thing over and over again. Just as a child in potty training, some Christians have to be encouraged or taught the same message over and over again. Some Christians just can't get it. Having a mind-set that prepares us to deal with God's children on their levels is important. One day these individuals will be delivered, and their stories will make a great testimony for someone else.

God uses our weaknesses to show himself strong in us, but then he uses that same situation to bless someone who might be challenged by the enemy. Christians are called to build people up and not tear them down. If God can use a recovered drug addict, alcoholic, sex offender, or thief, he can also use recovered homosexuals. Meeting people where they are means acknowledging that homosexuals are not born but practice by free will. Being born with certain attributes doesn't make a person a homosexual, but the person takes on the name once he or she acts on those unnatural feelings.

Unfortunately, those who feel strongly rooted in heterosexuality label those who appear different out of ignorance. Some guys are just feminine, but it's not fair to label them. Let us not condemn people as they go through their trials because we consider some struggles normal and others abnormal. Regardless of where people are in life, we have direct orders to love them. We don't have a heaven or hell to put anyone in, so it's not our place to do the judging.

Never forget or pretend to have forgotten that God says, "The way of a fool is right in his own eyes" (Prov. 12:15). "Every way of a man is right in his own eyes: but the LORD pondereth [weighted] the hearts" (Prov. 21:2). No matter how convenient it may be to justify ourselves, God sees the truth behind it all. So instead of taking matters into our own hands, let us look at every situation through his eyes: "By a new and living way, which he hath consecrated for us" (Heb. 10:20).

Chapter 12

The Controversy of Once Saved, Always Saved

Can a person truly lose his or her salvation? This topic seems to be the talk of many people in different denominations; perhaps it's the way some religions flow. This question goes deeper than the finite minds of humans. Therefore, in order to acquire the real truth of the matter, we must go to the source: the only absolute, omnipotent God. In spite of popular opinion, the only word that will stand in the end is the unadulterated word of God.

The term "fall away" in Hebrews 6:6 may give the impression that salvation can be lost, or the death-defying times mentioned in 2 Timothy 3 encourage the notion of losing one's salvation. The word *apostasy* may also insinuate the probability of saints no longer being saved, based on certain behavior patterns. It is for certain that there will be a falling away from the church because the word of God says so. Let's put the text in perspective, which is the key to understanding that salvation can't be lost.

For instance, Jesus says in John 10:28–29, "And I give unto them eternal life; and they shall never perish, neither shall any man pluck them out of my hand. My Father, which gave them me, is greater than all; and no man is able to pluck them out of my Father's hand." Hebrews

> Nevertheless the foundation of God standeth sure, having this seal, The Lord knoweth them that are his. (2 Tim. 2:19)

6:4–6 states, "For it is impossible for those who were once enlightened, and have tasted the heavenly gift, and were made partakers of the Holy Ghost, And have tasted the good word of God, and the powers of the world to come, If they shall fall away, to renew them again unto repentance."

Impossible is the incapability of something being done. Falling away is real, but not for those who are truly washed in the blood of the Lamb. Falling away or apostasy is defined as forsaking the faith. *Forsake* is an abandonment or rejection, which is not the same as backsliding. Backsliding leaves room for repentance, but turning away from the faith is revoking the gospel.

Some people profess to know him and consider themselves to be Christians without applying scripture to their lives. They are fully functioning in the local assembly in many auxiliaries, but the Bible teaches us in 1 Timothy 3:5 that some people are "having a form of godliness but denying the power thereof."

Some people only believe certain scriptures in the Bible, and others say the Old Testament is no longer valid. Some professed Christians only accept the red letters of the Bible (quotes of Jesus). If you've ever conversed with this group of individuals, you'll find it quite interesting how they can defend certain verses boldly but totally disregard others.

To make a statement suggesting that salvation can be lost is misleading. It would be more accurate to say that person was never saved. But who has God given the power to determine who is saved or who is not? It is a Christian's place to witness and present ourselves as living sacrifices before the world by revealing Christ. Jesus is the example, and so we should ask ourselves, "Did Jesus condemn people, or did he speak life to them by teaching the truth and offering salvation?" Christians will often sentence people to hell without grasping what God says about the matter of being long-suffering in 2 Peter 3:9.

A distinguished few believe that backsliding is a sure way of identifying an unsaved person. Again, no person is authorized to make that assessment. "Now if any man have not the Spirit of Christ, he is none of his" (Rom. 8:9). Only God can judge a person's service or make a determination whether or not a person is saved. The saints should simply be a voice for him, bridging two worlds.

How can we be a bridge, and what two worlds are we connecting? God is all Spirit, the unsaved person is operating in flesh, and the saved person is flesh possessing the Holy Spirit, directly connected to both.

"For the prophecy came not in old time by the will of man: but holy men of God spake as they were moved by the Holy Ghost" (2 Pet. 1:21). God miraculously speaks to his Spirit, residing in the saints and instructing the body how to witness to those disconnected. It's not our place to analyze another person's character, to

> Speak not evil one of another, brethren. He that speaketh evil of his brother, and judgeth his brother, speaketh evil of the law, and judgeth the law: but if thou judge the law, thou art not a doer of the law, but a judge. (James 4:11)

criticize, or even to inspect the spiritual fruit of others. We are simply called to witness. Let us not lose sight of this. The scripture says, "Ye shall know them by their fruits" (Matt. 7:16). These fruits are simply methods to help us recognize those who need our witnessing and to acknowledge when teachers are not teaching based on the revelation of God. We must refrain from sitting under their philosophy, but we should not place judgment on them. We mustn't forget that false teachers are people, and they need saving.

The Bible teaches how God used imperfect people to accomplish his mission. He never consented to sin but handled it in a loving way. Moses "spied an Egyptian smiting an Hebrew, one of his brethren. And he looked this way and that way, and when he saw that there was no man, he slew the Egyptian, and hid him in the sand" (Exod. 2:11–12). Yet God used Moses to carry out one of his greatest tasks, which was to lead His people out of the land of Egypt.

Let's review David's history: "a man after mine own heart, which shall fulfill all my will" (Acts 13:22). David committed adultery with Bathsheba and had her husband, Uriah, killed to cover his sin. As a result of sin, this child died shortly after birth. But God still blessed David and Bathsheba with four sons, one whose name was Solomon. "Sat Solomon upon the throne of David his father; and his kingdom was established greatly" (1 Kings 2:12). Both David and his son were imperfect men used by God. Solomon, the wisest man to ever live, was chosen by God (1 Kings 4:29–34). But Solomon disobeyed God by having many strange women. "And he had seven hundred wives, princesses, and three hundred concubines: and his wives turned away his heart" (1 Kings 11:3). We can't forget Jonah, who ran away from God. "Now the word of the LORD came unto Jonah … Arise, go to Nineveh, that great city, and cry against it; for their wickedness is come up before me. But Jonah rose up to flee unto Tarshish from the presence of the LORD" (Jon. 1:1–2). These flawed biblical individuals played a role in the plans of God. So how is it that the Almighty God could use people such as these, after proper guidance, while humans in our finiteness condemn people to hell? God had a purpose for these men, as he did imperfect women of the Bible. Although he used them, it didn't come without reprimanding. "For God sent not his Son into the world to condemn the world; but that the world through him might be saved" (John 3:17).

Jesus came on the scene with a different set of rules. He didn't override his Father but merely changed the guidelines in order to be used by God. Paul is a prime example of how Jesus operated. Paul was a Jew who was all about keeping the law, to the point of killing Christians. He functioned without heart, but Jesus is all about heart, which means Paul had to learn how to die to self and work under the principles of spirituality. Once Paul understood "that the righteousness of the law might be fulfilled in us, who walk not after the flesh, but after the Spirit" (Rom. 8:4), he became the man whom Jesus could truly use to encourage weak souls and witness to the lost. In fact, his name was changed from Saul to Paul. He approached the situation under the name Saul, but after an encounter with Satan, as described in Acts 13:6–9, he only went by the name Paul. Verse nine of Acts says, "Then Saul, [who also is called Paul] filled with the Holy Ghost, set his eyes on him." All Christians receive the gift of the Spirit, but there's a difference in having the Spirit and being filled with the Spirit. Chapter 9 in the book of Acts talks about Paul having the Spirit, but chapter 13 says he was filled with the Spirit. "Therefore if any man be in Christ, he is a new creature: old things are passed away; behold, all things are become new" (2 Cor. 5:17). For clarity, the Bible doesn't really say that God changed Saul's name to Paul, but this example simply acknowledges the convenience of the timing when he strictly went by the name Paul. Case in point, God can and will use all people who make themselves available.

For the most part, people probably don't wake up and decide to fall again into sin, but bit by bit Satan pulls them back into unrighteousness. They slowly lose focus and begin participating in activities from which the Lord had freed them. Think for an instant: if you took a minute to evaluate your life at this very moment, would you be a prime example of someone who has backslid at some point of your Christian life (lying, gossiping, judging, etc.)? No one can really judge another person because the examination is truly within one's self. Psalm 139 says, "Search me, O God." The operative word here is *me*. If you are saved, "grieve not the Holy Spirit of God, whereby ye are sealed unto the day of redemption" (Eph. 4:30). Furthermore, Paul teaches us in Galatians 6:1 that "if a man be overtaken in a fault, ye which are spiritual, restore such an one in the spirit of meekness [longsuffering, forgiving, etc.]; considering thyself, lest thou also be tempted."

Certain professions will place people in the eyes of the public, causing many of their shortcomings to be viewed more harshly than those whose sins are kept private. Is this fair? Does their position justify rumors or small talk about their lives? A celebrity addicted to drugs or alcohol is no different from your next-door neighbor who has addictions. An addiction is an attack of the enemy, regardless of who the victim might be. The prodigal son mentioned in Luke 15:11–32 is an example of how we fall into sin, but God's grace will lead us back to him. Let we who have answered the call of the Lord Jesus remain compassionate toward others. Let us live love to teach people the truth of our Lord Jesus Christ. If by chance an individual isn't saved but is simply religious, living love before such a person can plant a seed or lead him or her to Christ. Let us do our part as Christians and not play little gods.

Chapter 13

Sleeping Young Parents

Thoughts of growing up and leaving home consume the mind of the average child. "I'm grown" or "I can do what I want" are popular phrases young adults often embrace with a passion, but they have no idea what they really mean. Many of them don't know the difference between being grown and being a mature adult. To say, "I'm grown" is merely the world's way of making people responsible for themselves. Some are excited because the law says at twenty-one, an individual reaches the legal drinking age. Simply saying this doesn't makes a person responsible. To say, "I'm a mature adult" means a person is taking charge of his or her life, especially as a young parent—a role that takes adulthood to another level.

A young parent must learn how to renounce selfishness and practice putting the child first. This does not suggest putting children before the marriage relationship. In Genesis 2:24, God says, "Therefore shall a man leave his father and his mother, and shall cleave unto his wife: and they shall be one flesh." So, putting the child first deals with self-centeredness. For some parents this comes naturally, but for others putting a child first takes a lot of practice. Young parents are no longer learning life for themselves; they are learning how to live in a way that's best for a family. If you're new to parenting, things in your world are about to get real, and fast! Your own parents or guardians are there to help, but you have to learn how to make your own way through prayer and guidance from the Lord. God has entrusted a little life into your hands, which is a huge responsibility. You must make your family a priority. You've had a great time hanging out late with friends, taking spontaneous trips, and eating out all the time. Now you have a baby, so those things will have to be minimized. Sometimes date night might be a candlelit dinner at home after the baby is asleep, or the one night a week the baby is visiting grandparents. Perhaps you can make plans biweekly when the grandparents have the baby for the weekend, or whatever arrangements you may make. But you mustn't get angry with family because they won't keep the baby so you can go out three nights a week. The time has come to be young, mature adults. You'll want to take hold of the experience and enjoy it.

Some of you may have a spouse who has fallen asleep. How do you handle it? Pray, live love, and be nurturing. Will this be easy? Not always. God could move immediately, but he may allow you the opportunity to mature through this experience. Keep your eyes on him. Negative communication will affect the child, so be careful not to openly reveal your resentments.

Let us begin at home, where it starts, because the world is the result of trillions of homes that make up a community and then a city, which creates a county, shapes a state, and unites into a country, which in turn populates the whole world.

Children are blessings from God. They bring joy into our homes and grow up to continue blessing our homes with grandchildren. On the other hand, even under proper guidance, some children stray from the truth for various reasons. If they are brought up on the sure foundation of Jesus Christ, eventually they'll find their way back. When our children face life's storms, we should be supportive and not curse them. We shouldn't say "I'll be glad when they're gone" or "I'm counting down the days," although some children are rebellious and proud of it. This could lead their parents into feeling mentally exhausted from the effects of keeping them off drugs, out of jail, or simply alive. Raising children isn't always easy, but we can't give up on them. Many times they'll keep their problems locked inside and refuse to share them with someone who can help. They fail to see just how vulnerable they've become, and this makes their situations worse. Bullying is a good example of how our children are embarrassed to let anyone know that they are living in fear or shame. Let's not sit back and count the days before graduation. Instead, let's allow our children to see how sad we are that they're leaving but how happy we are about the success that lies ahead of them.

God loves children, and therefore it is not enough to simply provide for them physically and materially. We must also give them the most important part: love. It's wrong for us as parents to ignore the emotional needs of our children. Nourishing them emotionally is a part of the rearing process. "Train up a child in the way he should go: and when he is old, he will not depart from it" (Prov. 22:6). *Way* in this text is a means or method of doing a specific thing or taking a specific path. *Train* suggests guidance or steering to impact a person's behavior patterns. The most effective way to bring a significant change in the world is to begin at home with the word of God.

Chapter 14

Deliverance

Teaching about deliverance is easy for the teacher, but it's quite challenging for the student. The lecturers bring words of encouragement that can make a person feel motivated and strengthened. This is their responsibility as instructors. It is also their duty to educate with passion to enlighten their student's knowledge of Jesus Christ to the degree of promoting a change. The Bible teaches that Jesus is power; therefore, the power to change is within us. We have to learn about him to know how to connect with this power.

Unfortunately, souls are lacking awareness because some teachers fail to take this responsibility seriously. Perhaps they target certain people and fail to reach others. Teaching based on rumors doesn't get the messages of God to those who really need to hear from him. God is all-knowing; he doesn't need gossip to reach those who are broken.

If you're a teacher who resorts to this kind of teaching, you need to break free. How long you've been teaching or who your family members are in the church doesn't matter. Your allegiance is to the Lord, not to the local assembly. If God called you to teach as you say he did, rely on him to lead you so that you will operate under his will and not your own. If you are broken, begin your recovery with prayer and then go to your pastor for counseling. God will place people in your life who can help you, people from whom you can receive the wisdom they have to offer.

Everyone isn't teachable. Perhaps a reluctant few feel that they've experienced everything in life there is to know. No matter what situation or conversation comes up, they are always in the know. Is this you? Of course it's not you. But do you always have something to say? As Christians, we can't be unreachable, because it closes the door to God's spiritual blessings and maturity in Christ. Possibly some people are reachable but can't receive information from certain people. What does God have to say about that type of behavior? If the informant is a child of God, then you had better get your heart in the right place, because whether you receive it or not, God says, "So shall my word be that goeth forth out of my mouth: it shall not return unto me void, but it shall accomplish that which I please, and it shall prosper in the thing whereto I sent It" (Isa. 55:11). God uses whomever he wishes, even if you don't personally like the individual. In so many instances, God has set the table for two, so you can choose to eat or not eat, but either way his word will bless someone. Will you be blessed, or will the blessing go to the person next to you who overhears the conversation because you let it pass you by?

"For the time will come when they will not endure sound doctrine" (2 Tim. 4:3). A conclusion lies in the hearts of countless people, which gears them toward denying the truth. Even those who attend worship service on a regular basis are selective of biblical text. Preachers and teachers can bring the word of God according to scripture, yet so many people choose to believe only those verses that make life convenient for them. In spite of this falling world, all men called by God to preach or teach must be as Paul, who said, "My speech and my preaching was not with enticing words of man's wisdom, but in demonstration of the Spirit and of power: That your faith should not stand in the wisdom of men, but in the power of God" (1 Cor. 2:4–5).

Teaching should begin at home with our children, who should be taught strictly by the Bible. These ages are too crucial for us to fail at the most important task given to humankind by God. People are trapped in psychosomatic illnesses, Christians are backsliding, and billions are delusional because Satan has blinded them to the truth. We don't have time to entertain when we should be revealing Jesus Christ. The Bible teaches that everyone won't be saved; in fact, more souls will be lost than saved (Matt. 7:14). Fortunately, those individuals are in the hands of God. We must merely do what he has instructed us to do as pastors, teachers, husbands, wives, singles, leaders, and witnesses. God is not asking those who are spiritually sick to serve those who are not in Christ, but for those who are spiritually inclined to serve those who are sick.

Everyone has an opinion on certain matters. Politics and religion are the most controversial topics in all times. These debates bring about much uproar in the workplace, perhaps to the point of becoming arguments. At the conclusion of the discussion, have you ever found yourself replaying the conversation in your mind to prove yourself right? No one knows it all or has all of the answers; we must learn to be silent to keep peace, especially when the conversation is pointless. "In a multitude of words there wanteth (lack) not sin: but he that refraineth his lips is wise" (Prov. 10:19). "A soft answer turneth away wrath: but grievous words stir up anger. The tongue of the wise useth knowledge aright: but the mouth of fools poureth out foolishness" (Prov. 15:1–2). Let us break free of the know-it-all mentality, because it is not of God. We are called to holiness, which should be seen in our lifestyle, words, and the spiritual fruit we bear.

"This I say … Walk in the Spirit, and ye shall not fulfill the lust of the flesh. For the flesh lusteth against the Spirit, and the Spirit against the flesh" (Gal. 5:16–17). Open marriages, bisexuality, lesbianism, and homosexuality have become the choices of today's humanity. This may be true for millions, but not so for a child of God. As Christians, we know that Jesus has called his people to something greater than physical satisfaction. "He [Jehovah] which made them at the beginning made them male and female" (Matt. 19:4). Your birth recorded in heaven holds the facts of your real identity. "The thief cometh not, for but to steal" (John 10:10). Know who you are so that the devil can't steal your true identity. God has instructed his children to flee sexual sin. He puts emphasis on the sin of unnatural affections, which is an outrage according to Romans 1:26–27. "Marriage is honourable in all, and the bed undefiled: but whoremongers and adulterers God will judge" (Heb. 13:4).

Christians are not called to sexual greed by God, but to be faithful to one husband or one wife. Why marry if you are still open to others? Why commit to one person when you haven't dealt with your sexual addiction? Why invite STDs into your home? Why not stay single until you've allowed God to deliver you? Are you selfish? You might be saying, "I am single, and I will remain single so that I may enjoy myself without the guilt from hurting someone." Well, you may not feel guilty, but God says, "Flee fornication. Every sin that a man doeth is without the body; but he that committeth fornication sinneth against his own body" (1 Cor. 6:18).

For decades, preachers have taught the word of God to the best of their ability. Many of them study day in and day out to bring "the sincere milk of the word, that ye may grow thereby" (1 Pet. 2:2). Unfortunately, they continue to see the same behaviors from those who claim to be new creations in Christ, and this grieves some preachers and pastors and discourages others. Why utilize time and energy trying to lead people to Christ when the congregation isn't listening? Why not throw in the towel?

They may feel as though they're not accomplishing anything, which they may not on their own strength. But they are reaching many unsaved people through the power of God. It's because of Jesus's sacrifice for humankind that the preacher will plant the seed and another will water it, "but God ... giveth the increase" (1 Cor. 3:7). Therefore, "be not weary in well doing. And if any man obey not our word by this epistle [letter/message], note that man, and have no company with him, that he may be ashamed. Yet count him not an enemy, but admonish him as a brother" (2 Thess. 3:13–15).

No one's disobedience should be recognized in the mouths of busybodies, but only by actual truths. If the accusers lie about another person's actions, the faultfinders are no better than the one in fault. Let us not take part in bearing tales, because God is not pleased. Don't allow the enemy to keep you in bondage. The gift of power is in you; by his power, free yourselves. The enemy has placed some young preachers in the midst of greedy, false, selfish, or carnal pastors to corrupt their hearts. Many new preachers become cynical. Some turn against the gospel, and others concentrate on condemning preachers and pastors instead of spreading the good news of Jesus Christ. Only a faithful few have been able to break free of the enemy's trap and serve the Lord in relationship first.

Those who are incarcerated are often introduced to Christ for the first time. While they're free, it's hard for them to stand still long enough to receive what God has to say, especially because so many distractions are present in ordinary life. A preacher's love for people is perhaps more crucial than he realizes.

There are many opinions about what the most important jobs in the world might be. Parents, teachers, presidents of the United States, scientists, inventors, and others have been named as having the most significant responsibilities. Humanists are mainly concerned about human values, but Christians are mostly interested in the soul of mankind. "That which is born of the flesh is flesh and that which is born of the Spirit is spirit" (John 3:6). The roles of parents, teachers, and the president are critical for mankind because they provide guidance at different levels among the land of the living. Pastors and preachers are the mouthpieces of God not only to provide guidance in the flesh, but deliverance for the soul. Therefore, be encouraged. In the Gospel of John 17, Jesus prayed for his people.

> And now come I to thee and these things I speak in the world, that they might have my joy fulfilled in themselves. I have given them thy word; and the world hath hated them, because they are not of the world, even as I am not of the world. I pray not that thou shouldest take them out of the world, but that thou shouldest keep them from the evil. They are not of the world, even as I am not of the world. Sanctify them through thy truth: thy word is truth. As thou hast sent me into the world, even so have I also sent them into the world. And for their sakes I sanctify myself, that they also might be sanctified through the truth. Neither pray I for these alone, but for them also which shall believe on me through their word. (John 17:13–20)

Chapter 15

Getting Back to the Basics

The role of a Christian is to glorify God in all things. He has equipped every saint by his divine power with the ability to function in the flesh spiritually. His power is so magnificent that it can't be generated without a relationship with him, because there wouldn't be any spiritual connection. A unique preparation period requires persistence for a person to obtain a genuine bond with Christ. Peter was quite the example to present such specific measures and to have an unbelievable relationship with Jesus, considering he denied Jesus. But after his resurrection, Peter became one of the most persistent disciples of the twelve. In 2 Peter 1:5–7, he writes, "Add to your faith virtue; and to virtue knowledge; and to knowledge temperance; and to temperance patience; and to patience godliness; and to godliness brotherly kindness; and to brotherly kindness charity." He goes on to say in verse eight, "If these things be in you, and abound, they make you that ye shall neither be barren [unproductive] nor unfruitful in the knowledge of our Lord Jesus Christ."

"Stir up the gift of God, which is in thee" (2 Tim. 1:6). Paul counseled Timothy, "Neglect not the gift that is in thee" (1 Tim. 4:14). What is this gift of great significance? Well, the gifts of God come in different forms. The gift of Jesus lives in us by way of the Holy Spirit, so we can walk in peace, can operate in the truth, live righteously, resist the devil, embrace eternal life, and reveal the living word of God to the world. Also, gifts of tangible and intangible talents have been given to us by God to use as tools in service. Furthermore, we have the gifts of

God's spiritual fruit (Gal. 5:22–23). God "hath given unto us all things that pertain unto life and godliness, through the knowledge of him that hath called us to glory and virtue" (2 Pet. 1:3). "Therefore, we are fully equipped to run the race that is set before us. Looking unto Jesus, the author and finisher of our faith" (Heb. 12:1–2).

Let us. The word *let* is a permissive term. It means to consciously allow something to happen or take place. *Us* gives reference to the body of Christ. Below are a few "let us" texts according to scripture, which are possible through the omnipotence of God. However, let's not forget that people are imperfect beings (but the souls of the saints are kept by the sovereignty of God). Therefore, with all diligence:

- Let us therefore cast off the works of darkness, and let us put on the armour of light. (Rom. 13:12)
- Let us be free … If the Son therefore shall make you free, ye shall be free indeed. (John 8:36)
- Let us walk honestly, as in the day; not in rioting and drunkenness, not in chambering and wantonness, not in strife and envying. (Rom. 13:14)
- Let us not therefore judge one another any more: but judge this rather, that no man put a stumblingblock or an occasion to fall in his brother's way. (Rom. 14:13)
- Let us therefore follow after the things which make for peace, and things wherewith one may edify another. (Rom. 14:19)
- Neither let us commit fornication, as some of them committed. (1 Cor. 10:8)
- Neither let us tempt Christ, as some of them also tempted. (1Cor. 10:9)
- Let us cleanse ourselves from all filthiness of the flesh and spirit, perfecting holiness in the fear of God. (2 Cor. 7:1)
- If we live in the Spirit, let us also walk in the Spirit. (Gal. 5:25)
- Let us not be desirous of vain glory, provoking one another, envying one another. (Gal. 5:26)
- Let us not be weary in well doing: for in due season we shall reap, if we faint not. (Gal. 6:9)

- As we have therefore opportunity, let us do good unto all men, especially unto them who are of the household of faith. (Gal. 6:10)
- Let us not sleep, as do others; but let us watch and be sober. (1 Thess. 5:6)
- Let us, who are of the day, be sober, putting on the breastplate of faith and love; and for an helmet, the hope of salvation. (1 Thess. 5:8)
- And having food and raiment let us therefore be content. (1 Tim. 6:8)
- Seeing then that we have a great high priest, that is passed into the heavens, Jesus the Son of God, let us hold fast our profession. (Heb. 4:14)
- Let us therefore come boldly unto the throne of grace, that we may obtain mercy, and find grace to help in time of need. (Heb. 4:16)
- Let us hold fast the profession of our faith without wavering; [for he is faithful that promised]. (Heb. 10:23)
- Let us lay aside every weight, and the sin which doth so easily beset us. (Heb. 12:1)
- Let us have grace, whereby we may serve God acceptably with reverence and godly fear. (Heb. 12:28)
- Let us offer the sacrifice of praise to God continually, that is, the fruit of our lips giving thanks to his name. (Heb. 13:15)
- Let us not love in word, neither in tongue; but in deed and in truth. (1 John 3:18)
- Let us love one another: for love is of God; and every one that loveth is born of God, and knoweth God. (1 John 4:7)
- Let us be glad and rejoice, and give honour to him: for the marriage of the Lamb is come, and his wife hath made herself ready. (Rev. 19:7)

Let us make ourselves ready for the big day. We can start today by cleaning up our lives to make marriage as appealing as possible, and to invite as many people who are willing to attend. For certain, the cleaning process for most people will be difficult. The world has become captivating to so many minds, to the point of addiction. Not to mention the tremendous number of people dealing with anxiety, living in fear, and dealing with controlling and abusive spouses. Children are faced with bullying, peer pressure, and thoughts of suicide.

Getting ready for the big day and making the invitation attractive to guests is a task that only Jesus (the Great I AM) can conquer. Therefore, the church must allow Jesus to execute his master plan in these earthen vessels that he has called out of darkness to be a light for those who are still living in darkness. "Verily, verily, I say unto you, He that believeth on me, the works that I do shall he do also; and greater works than these shall he do" (John 14:12). "For as we have many members in one body, and all members have not the same office: So we, being many, are one body in Christ, and every one members one of another. Having then gifts differing according to the grace that is given to us" (Rom. 12:4–6). No position or status matters in the body of Christ because gifts are given for his glorification and his purpose. The work that is required of God's people needs to be manifested, not only in the way a person lives but also in the way saints operate in their gifts. "For ye are bought with a price: therefore glorify God in your body, and in your spirit, which are God's" (1 Cor. 6:20). He has the right to use His children as he pleases to reach those who are lost, those who are struggling to break free from strongholds, and those who are seeking direction in life.

People who exaggerate the truth fail to realize that they're still telling lies. Some racists live in denial with the notion that the hatred in their hearts is somehow nonexistent. The world is spiritually dark, and people are dying. Imagine the great depths of space and the millions of rays of starlight that exist in it as a reflection from the sun. Metaphorically, the members of Christ are like the many stars in space shining to enlighten the world of salvation. This amazing light is symbolic of the Son of God, which is how the saints are empowered. As people of faith, we are called to service and not to be served. "If our gospel be hid, it is hid to them that are lost. In whom the god of this world hath blinded the minds of them which believe not, lest the light of the glorious gospel of Christ, who is the image of God, should shine unto them" (2 Cor. 4:3–4). Jesus gave himself to save the world, "leaving us an example, that ye should follow his steps" (1 Pet. 2:21). "Ye are the light of the world. A city that is set on an hill cannot be hid" (Matt. 5:14). Therefore, "Let your light so shine before men, that they may see your good works, and glorify your Father which is in heaven" (Matt. 5:16).

The light of God can be hidden by some behaviors, which may or may not be considered a small thing. Commenting on another person's appearance, financial status, physical abilities, or personal possessions can be hurtful. It is important for the body of Christ that "no corrupt communication proceed out of your mouth, but that which is good to the use of edifying, that it may minister grace unto the hearers" (Eph. 4:29). Even if it's a whisper, you never know who may hear what is said. Hurting a sinner can cause him or her to denounce Christianity. For those who criticize, be very careful, because even if no one else hears the conversation, God does. "Therefore thou art inexcusable [no excuse], O man, whosoever thou art that judgest: for wherein thou judgest another, thou condemnest thyself; for thou that judgest doest the same things" (Rom. 2:1). Although this text is a reference to the Jews judging the Gentiles for their paganism, it still applies to us today.

The word *man* in Romans 2:1 is used interchangeably. Apparently, there has been some confusion with the usage of this word in the Bible. For argument's sake, let's clarify the true meaning of the word. *Man* in the Bible is used to give reference to mankind or human beings of either gender. It does not suggest that homosexuality is permissible. God made this absolutely clear in the Old and New Testaments (Lev. 20:13; Rom. 1:24–28). God is warning against judging others, and one sin isn't better than another. But unlike any other sin, he called same-sex relationships an outrage. Please, let's not get caught up in these things so that we may remain in fellowship with the Lord Jesus Christ. How can we pray for the world when we are out of communion with him? Let us not forget that consequences are ordered by God for unrighteousness.

For instance, when water leaves the clouds, it will fall to the ground or surface as rain, fog, sleet, hail, dew, or snow. When we sin, it will cost us something. Many of us face rainy lives, and once the rain comes, it pours. Sometimes we only suffer a little, such as with the dew, but the lives of others are cloudy, perhaps as thick as the fog. Willfully sinning or having a heart of self-satisfaction is playing with the justice of God, which is a dangerous thing.

The ignorance of this world has brought about deception, confusion, and false information, causing some people to live in uncertainty. They don't have the direction of God through Jesus, so they are looking for anyone who may appear to have the answers. Those who profess to be Christians but have no real knowledge of God are deceiving millions of people every day.

Scientists may be so entangled in facts that they can't perceive the truth of how scientific findings came about. For this reason, they are without the understanding that brings it all together. The mere thought of trying to manipulate God's unique creation of reproduction is delusional. It is a sure way to bring more disorder to humanity in health issues, psychosomatic complaints, or purely unpredictable conditions in the human body.

Explore Stem Cells reported on their web page concerning "Current Research for Same Sex Reproduction."

> The techniques purported to allow same-sex reproduction have yet to be successful but they do hold promise. They include methods of cellular reprogramming and even techniques such as artificial chromosomes. While they have not been shown to work at present, they do hold potential for the future of same-sex reproduction. One particular technique involves the creation of sperm from human stem cells. In a recent experiment, bone marrow stem cells were extracted from men and they were then triggered into spermatogonia. These cells are able to develop into immature sperm cells. The experiment was widely reported in the news but has not yet been published or successfully replicated (Murnaghan, 2017).

People of faith mustn't turn toward the way of the world but remain "stand fast in the Lord" (Phil. 4:1). Neither should we feel frustration over how the world chooses to live, because it is not the responsibility of

Christians to change anyone but simply to present the love of Christ to them. God didn't call saints to prey on other Christians or sinners, but to pray for each other. As individuals (whether Christians or sinners), we make decisions based on what we know, but the Christian will be held accountable by God.

Once the choice is made by someone to accept Jesus as God's Son, it is that person's responsibility is to learn about him (Matt. 11:29). Maintaining godly excellence isn't hard to do if Jesus is our choice and not our goal. There is a difference between our working for God and people experiencing Christ in us. Getting back to the basics simply means we must be about Christ, instead of merely talking about him. The average person will watch what we do versus what we say, so let's live the experience before the world to give them the best HD movie of Jesus's life on earth. This example will follow them for the rest of their lives so that they too may live the experience.

Chapter 16

We Can't Give Up Now

How many people do you know who have given up on something or someone? Many individuals have made a choice to let go of bad habits, give up on relationships, quit school, and stop trying to succeed. Is it a good idea to give up on people who are seeking help? Perhaps the person needing help doesn't honestly appear to be trying to get off drugs, and the struggle of hanging in there with him is taking a toll. Maybe the marriage is no longer worth the fight. And suppose a demanding boss fails to see the workload is more than one person can possibly handle. What should our approach be?

The Bible teaches that Satan is a powerful force, which makes life difficult, especially for Christians. "For we wrestle not against flesh and blood, but against principalities, against powers, against the rulers of the darkness of this world, against spiritual wickedness in high places" (Eph. 6:12). These things may be true of the devil, however people of faith shouldn't focus on issues caused by a power of darkness, but on the solution made possible by the power of Elohim, GOD … El Shaddai, the ALMIGHTY GOD … El Elyon, the MOST HIGH GOD. In other words, the name of Jesus. "If God be for us, who can be against us?" (Rom. 8:31).

Now isn't the time to give up on lost souls. It is time to show the world just how great God is by allowing his will to be done. How?

> Building up yourselves on your most holy faith,
> praying in the Holy Ghost, Keep yourselves in the

love of God, looking for the mercy of our Lord Jesus
Christ unto eternal life. And of some have compassion,
making a difference: And others save with fear, pulling
[snatching] them out of the fire; hating even the garment
spotted by flesh. (Jude 1:20–23)

For it is God [Elohim in Spirit] which worketh in you
both to will and to do of his good pleasure. (Phil. 2:13)

I now write unto you; in both which I stir up your
pure minds by way of remembrance: That ye may be
mindful of the words which were spoken before by the
holy prophets and of the commandment of the apostles
of the Lord and Saviour. (2 Pet. 3:1–2)

The world's perception of spirituality is broad and unrelated to
faith. Basically, an unfortunate number of people believe that each
person lives his or her life based on each one's opinion of life and death.
The truth holds no barrier to their actions, only self-evaluation rules.
God is merely a higher power to so many people, and so teasing about
the Bible or the holiness of God is easy when Christianity isn't real to
them.

Now isn't the time for spiritual unconsciousness. Seminars and
meetings, for example, typically put people to sleep. Some parts are
interesting and other parts are boring, so
people begin nodding or fidgeting with things
to stay awake. Some people find this true in
Christianity as well. Church services, for one,
cause people to lose focus because they feel the
services are too long.

> Submit yourselves to every ordinance of man for the Lord's sake. (1 Peter 2:13)

As a result, some people elect to only attend one-hour services on
Sunday. Try eating one physical meal
a week and then evaluating how the
body responds. Failing to eat a snack
(any form of Bible study), drink water
(having a prayer life), or having a

> "Wherefore take unto you the whole armour of God, that ye may be able to withstand in the evil day" (Eph. 6:13)

piece of fruit or juice (praise and worship) daily would make it impossible to function properly. How can a child of God neglect spiritual nourishment and be prepared to face the evils of this world? The battle will be lost every time. Why? Physical and spiritual battles belong to God, but how can a person call on the Lord God to fight when they don't have a relationship or fellowship in place?

Jesus told the Samaritan woman, "But the hour cometh, and now is, when the true worshippers shall worship the Father in spirit and in truth: for the Father seeketh such to worship him. God is a Spirit: and they that worship him must worship him in spirit and in truth" (John 4:23–24). "He is a rewarder of them that diligently seek him" (Heb. 11:6). "Looking diligently lest any man fail" (Heb. 12:15). Devoting quality time to spiritual growth is the key to standing firm, which allows Jesus to move freely through the church.

We can take precautionary measures to stand against the enemy because he is on his job to hinder God's work. He uses anger, discouragement, low self-esteem, impatience, anxiety, depression, addictions, and many other hindrances to slow down spiritual progress. He uses Christians against each other by finding these mind-sets funny or a means for carrying on comical conversations. On the contrary, those who laugh are unknowingly giving Satan a place to hold office in their lives.

> To whom ye forgive any thing, I forgive also: for if I forgave any thing, to whom I forgave it, for your sakes forgave I it in the person of Christ; Lest Satan should get an advantage of us. (2 Cor. 2:10-11)

The Bible teaches that Satan is the master deceiver. He uses material things as a distraction to stop Christians from making godly interests a priority and to keep the sinner happy and satisfied. "Love not the world, neither the things that are in the world. If any man love the world, the love of the Father is not in him" (1 John 2:15). Failing to forgive is another distraction to prevent God's work from going forward: "if ye forgive not men their trespasses, neither will your Father forgive your trespasses" (Matt. 6:15).

It's easy to say something to avoid the wiles of the devil. But the only way to keep him from getting the best of us is by staying close to Jesus. There's nothing amusing about being used by the enemy. Being used by Satan will take away the opportunity to be a servant of God. Seek help to restrain from Satan's strongholds so that you'll no longer be a tool for evil.

Unfortunately, Satan also uses sensitive moments to hinder the love of God. Negligence is often camouflaged as thoughtfulness to pacify a broken person. Troubled people seeking compassion don't need insincere conversations to relieve them of their painful situation. Satan uses this tactic to keep Christians from expressing genuine love toward those who need it most. This isn't to say that Christians will always feel upbeat and ready for deep discussions. But remember, meeting the needs of others requires our undivided attention, and if we can't devote our time totally to their needs, we should let them know. Tell them so they will be made aware of the level of attentiveness of the conversation and won't have any hard feelings. Honesty is always the best policy.

Christians simply can't give up now because people who are trapped in situations they can't control—such as human trafficking, the abuse of children, and mental disturbance—are depending on the saints to pray for them. People living in fear and feeling they have nowhere to turn are counting on God's children to lift them up in prayer.

Compassion is needed for our children. Many of them have never had a caring parent to teach them about life, resulting in them falling into a life of crime. They are trusting that someone will pray for them because they don't know how. Some Christians are conscious of the society's spiritual position and are diligently praying, going out in the field, and setting up programs to help those who feel desperate. Still, many Christians are complacent, with little or no regard for others.

For those who fall into this category: wake up! When God looks at you, he wants to see himself. As long as he is seeing you, you are out of sync spiritually with God. The body of Christ is a group of people working together for one common cause, which is to serve God. We can serve God by allowing Jesus to move from one person to the next, healing one and saving another, rescuing some and comforting whoever is in need. He is a ransom for sinners. He has sealed the redeemed until the day of redemption.

The members of Christ are merely vessels for him to work through, but he can only work through a person if the temple is in good working condition. For instance, have you ever tried to fix something with a broken piece of equipment? Eventually, you'll give up, or you'll replace the broken piece of equipment. Are you spiritually in working condition? We must search ourselves to see if Jesus can use us to reach out to people seeking him or to those who are broken. Are you in working condition? William McDowell was on the right track when he wrote the song "I Give Myself Away." The words say a lot about who we should be as Christians, and it expresses the passionate side of being God's servants.

What does it mean to give yourself away for God's purpose? It's not just to serve on a committee in the house of prayer, but to really give yourself away. What would that require a person to give up? "Let him deny himself, and take up his cross daily, and follow me" (Luke 9:23). *Let* in this text gives humans the choice of free will. For instance, people apply for jobs, go to work, and attend on required days. They don't have to go on time or complete the work, but they will if they want to keep their jobs.

People seek Christ because they want to. God wants willing participants, not those who feel that all is lost if they're not running things or involved at a higher level. To be a servant of God suggests being called by Christ and freed from sin. Denying oneself is acknowledging that all things are only possible through Jesus (John 15:5). "For he that is called in the Lord, being a servant, is the Lord's freeman: likewise also he that is called, being free, is Christ's servant" (1 Cor. 7:22). This passage isn't solely for the saint's inheritance, but for contributing to the kingdom of God through service. Therefore, "Brethren, let every man, wherein he is called, therein abide with God" (1 Cor. 7:24).

The enemy will use any method possible to work against the body of Christ, such as by making vindictiveness appear as a normal reaction, or by making revenge the proper approach to address spitefulness. He has already blinded teenagers to believe that insulting others is okay, bashing music is cool, and accepting safe sex instead of abstinence is fine. He has persuaded young girls to sell their bodies for money, and some have continued into adulthood. He has cultivated society into accepting evil books and movies as innocent entertainment. He has corrupted the minds of men to abandon their responsibilities as husbands and fathers.

Even women are seeking to control their husbands, which is not within the order of God.

Now is not the time to give up, because it is unmistakably clear that the enemy isn't going to give up deceiving the world. Unfortunately, the world can't see God "turning the cities of Sodom and Gomorrha into ashes condemned them with an overthrow, making them an ensample into those that after should live ungodly" (2 Pet. 2:6). The enemy continues to deceive mankind into making ungodly laws that are pleasurable to many people. The devil is so clever that he has fooled people into believing that their bondage is freedom.

Plenty of work lies ahead, but many obstacles stand in the way. Always remember:

> The LORD is my light and my salvation; whom shall I fear? the LORD is the strength of my life; of whom shall I be afraid? (Ps. 27:1)

> Fear thou not; for I am with thee: be not dismayed; for I am thy God: I will strengthen thee; yea, I will help thee; yea, I will uphold thee with the right hand of my righteousness. (Isa. 41:10)

> Therefore, my beloved brethren, be ye stedfast, unmoveable, always abounding in the work of the Lord, forasmuch as ye know that your labour is not in vain in the Lord. (1 Cor. 15:58)

> As every man hath received the gift, even so minister the same one to another, as good stewards of the manifold grace of God. (1 Pet. 4:10)

> Now unto him that is able to keep you from falling, and to present you faultless before the presence of his glory with exceeding joy, To the only wise God our Saviour, be glory and majesty, dominion and power, both now and forever. Amen. (Jude 1:24)

Chapter 17

Live Love

Love is the end result of everything Christians are called to do in our lifetime. It is the sum total of lessons taught, songs sung, service rendered, and sermons preached. Most importantly, love is the life lived by every single person in the body of Christ. For instance, consider the story of a little girl playing with an eight-month-old baby. When the baby would say, "Da-da-goo-goo," the little girl would say, "Da-da-goo-goo," too. The little girl's mother looked over at her and said, "The baby doesn't know how to talk, but you do. How will she learn how to talk if you mimic her instead of teaching her?" Love dwells within every Christian, but if the saints of God mimic the world and fail to live love before them, how will they know that love exists, let alone understand there is something better than what the world has to offer?

Unfortunately, we are not in a good place as an ultimate resource to show the world what love is. The cross is the perfect example of love. It was suffering, sacrifice, selflessness, and the total giving of oneself—the very acts that saints are called to do. Spreading the word of God all over the world isn't enough; someone has to bring the word to life. The world can't comprehend the wisdom or revelation of God's holy and divine word; the people who are called by his name must define the scriptures by living a certain lifestyle.

To clarify this statement, the terminology for lifestyle is used in the singular form. A Christian has only one way to live love, and that is according to what God has already said. We need to grasp that Jesus's coming was all about reconciling humankind to himself through the amazing gospel of the Trinity.

There was an eternal reign before time when no evil existed. Everything was good and working in complete harmony. But now, we have principalities, powers, rulers of darkness, and spiritual wickedness in high places causing great havoc in the world and in the lives of mankind. (Eph. 6:12). Through the saints, God wants to revive his people and save those who lost their way (1 John 4:16). How is it done?

> Forasmuch then as Christ hath suffered for us in the flesh, arm yourselves likewise with the same mind: for he that hath suffered in the flesh hath ceased from sin. (1 Pet. 4:1)

> I beseech you therefore, brethren, by the mercies of God, that ye present your bodies a living sacrifice, holy, acceptable unto God, which is your reasonable service. (Rom. 12:1)

> I made myself servant unto all, that I might gain the more. (1 Cor. 9:19)

In order to live love by the standards of God, we can't show favoritism. "God commendeth his love toward us, in that, while we were yet sinners, Christ died for us" (Rom. 5:8). God being power and love gave himself direct orders to love us unconditionally. If we can only take hold of our spirituality (completely outside of the flesh), we will magnify God's power greatly throughout the whole world. Our God is greater than any other god or power in existence, but we limit his abilities to function through us in the immeasurable supremacy that he is. Sleeping Christians prevent the world from seeing just how great he is.

When we allow God to revive us into the spiritual beings that we are and suppress the flesh, words can't explain his mighty works that will go forward. How do we get to this place as a community of God-fearing people? How can we face a dying world and rise above it? How do we translate this revelation to our children who have not yet developed wisdom? We accomplished this by living love. Talking is overrated; it's time to start living by the example of Jesus Christ.

When we teach one thing but our lifestyle says something different, this is called a hindrance. God has called us to something much greater than walking by the flesh. His sovereignty gives us the ability to work through him, who is incapable of failing. His word says if we walk not in the counsel of the ungodly, nor stand in the way of sinners, nor sit in the seat of the scornful but delight ourselves in him, then we are like trees planted by the rivers of water. He says we shall bring forth fruit in our individual seasons, and whatsoever we do shall prosper (Ps. 1:1–3).

Do we really know who we have working in us? He is the Spirit of God, the same God who existed before there was a heaven or earth, who created humans in his own image and made himself known as the Almighty God, the Prince of Peace, Jehovah Elohim, Jehovah-jireh, Jehovah-nissi, Jehovah-rapha, Jehavoh-shalom, Jehovah-shammah, etc. He then took all of these names, rolled them up into one (Jesus), and implanted himself in the womb of a woman to be born in a world of sinners, to dwell among us. Love came down from glory to live among unworthy people and demonstrate his love through the cross. Not only that, but through his love and by the cross, he gave himself as ransom for the sin of humankind.

Now, "I am crucified with Christ: nevertheless I live; yet not I, but Christ liveth in me: and the life which I now live in the flesh I live by the faith of the Son of God, who loved me, and gave himself for me" (Gal. 2:20). Living love isn't a physical act. Jesus came to dwell among us in the flesh so that he could become the ultimate sacrifice. That's who we are: spiritual beings dwelling in the flesh (earthly vessels) until God calls us home. We will return to our spiritual state and leave the flesh to return to the dust of the earth. We must study to learn how to operate according to our nature. As the body of Christ, we have to wake up from our slumber and get busy living love, because this dying world is depending on us.

Living love requires stepping out of the box. What does that mean? Servicing the Lord isn't confined to people of a certain class or financial status. We should never have cliques in the body of Christ. God has a place for people who have a heart like his, seek to have a heart like his, or work at having a heart like his. Mistreatment isn't always done purposely. Some people are caught up in defining themselves, so they make bad listeners, supporters, or friends.

Chapter 18

The Question Is ...

If the world is dying and the church is sick, where do people go, or whom do they seek for help? This spiritual sickness in the church has made us vulnerable to the culture, too intimidated to challenge world views, paralyzed by the government, and broken by the direction this generation has chosen. Living in defeat has consumed many of God's people because we have somehow forgotten the hope of Christ and have given up. Sure, there are gospel television shows and Christian radio talk shows to get the word out that Jesus lives, and countless local assemblies are teaching the message of John 3:16 to anyone who will listen. But what about the church? Revival programs are held annually to revive the body of Christ, but are we applying the information?

Is the church simply too weak in spiritual strength to do and be who God has called us to be? Just look at the shape this world is in. God told his people to humble themselves and turn from their wicked ways, and then he will heal the land. The Great Physician doesn't need medicine or the hands of humans, but by his word alone can heal all illnesses. Whether the illness is of the body or mind, he can make it whole. All we have to do is awaken from our sleep and stir up the gift of love by his power that is within us, the power to stand firm, the power of deliverance, the power to shine, and the power that's of the most-high God that miraculously saves souls. He is the power that makes up energy, the neutrons and protons that evolutionists say were at the beginning of time. It is his power that exists in eternity and time at once, which makes wisdom and knowledge evidence of his characteristics. Even his name, El Elyon, means highest. If we have the highest form of power living within us, what can keep us down? What can stand against us? What power of darkness or spiritual wickedness is able to move us? We are more powerful than we know not because of who we are, but for the simple reason that he lives within us.

Stop and think. We have an unbeatable force watching over us, protecting us, keeping us, and making a path for us. Why won't we let Jesus be himself in us? Do we think he will fail or somehow not succeed? Are we looking at this Christian journey through human eyes instead of spiritual eyes? Something has to be working against us, which we have given power to overtake our subconscious mind. Resulting in our inability to follow through.

When unforeseen circumstances come into our lives, we have to somehow find balance in it all. Sometimes we become mentally motionless, which is precisely when the enemy will attack. Therefore, while others are healing from losing a loved one, recovering from a difficult time, or dealing with a sick loved one, the rest of the body of Christ should be standing in the gap to lift them up. We must take care of one another first so that we are undivided when we face the world.

We can't give the devil a place to work in the church. Why is it so hard for us to help people where they are in life? Why won't we look at the problem instead of the person? We should be diligently praying for those who are strung out and passionately praying to God for the girls caught up in prostitution. Do we see people culturally instead of by cause and effect? People are suffering deeply and need our help, not our criticism. Let us approach the broken with caution; if their situation is too sensitive to make contact, we can always pray and then pray some more.

We must prioritize and focus on the right things. Criticizing people or other Christians about how they pray isn't the issue at hand. Some people teach that we shouldn't say, Father, Lord, God, or Jesus too many times while we pray. They compare it to talking with a friend or spouse and repeating their name in nearly every sentence. People are dying, and others are trapped in sin—but we're concerned about how many times we should call the Father's name?

The model prayer isn't repetitive in calling names, but it's a model.

Calling the Lord repeatedly makes it more personal and precious to many, and this shouldn't be judged by others. Teaching how to pray is okay, but not to the degree of taking away a person's individuality. Satan is a trickster who uses distractions at any level to hinder progress in the kingdom of God. Let's not fall for it. Instead, let us prioritize by attending some form of Bible study to learn how to witness, how to pray for others, how to teach, and how to live by example. Always remember that God doesn't need us, but he wants to use our gifts and talents for his purpose.

Agape is most effective when it's doing what it does by the source from which it derives its existence. People spend quality time trying to give love, show love, or perhaps spread love through their efforts. For the flesh to produce such a love as this is unattainable, and therefore this amazing gift can only be possible if God delivers it through his people. "If we love one another, God dwelleth in us, and his love is perfected in us. Hereby [as a result of] know we that we dwell in him, and he in us, because he hath given us of his Spirit" (1 John 4:12–13).

Can people truly say they are mature in Christ when they fail to love by God's standards? Can people honestly believe that God encourages hate? Those who believe that sin is okay as long as the cause is due to spiritual immaturity have a serious problem. This concept leads people down the wrong path, which could explain why we see so much hate, deception, and cohabitation.

People who are being taught that God is a forgiving God, but who are not taught any accountability or consequences for their actions, are being misled. The same goes for people who feel they can dislike others because of their looks, the way they might walk, or their past sins. Grace is a gift that can't be measured by personal standards. Although sin is not okay, God is merciful. The question is, do we justify sin in our minds? Are we verbally forgiving but remaining angry in our hearts? "If a man say, I love God, and hateth his brother, he is a liar: for he that loveth not his brother whom he hath seen, how can he love God whom he hath not seen?" (1 John 4:20).

God's children are not resistant to pain; at times living love for certain people after they've hurt you may be difficult. The key is knowing how to get past it. We can fall down on our knees and ask

Elnora Wilson

Jesus to release himself within us so that we can forgive others the way he forgives us. None of us are perfect, so let's allow Jesus (love) to work through us so the world may know that God is alive, and he lives within us.

Chapter 19

Teachers, Faculty, and Staff

Teachers, faculty, and staff are some of the world's most trusted people. Parents everywhere send their children to spend forty hours a week with them to academically prepare their minds for the workforce. Due to the size of the student body, many days teachers probably feel as though the weight of the world is on their shoulders.

Teachers face a tremendous responsibility every time they walk into the school. A community of children congregates in the school forty hours per week for nine to ten months out of the year. Every child commuting in the hallways each day has a story. Some stories are happy, and some are sad. Others are stories of fear and a few are tragic. Whatever is going on in children's hearts will be played out at school. They will react in different ways, reflecting their stories.

Teachers, faculty, and staff have to understand each child individually to meet his or her needs. Bad grades may be the result of a troubled child, leading the student to be distracted and unfocused. Counselors should be educated in every area of child psychology in order to connect with the students to deal with the issues and help get them back on track academically.

It is evident that all teachers aren't Christians, and therefore all counseling sessions aren't based on biblical standards. The faculty members in schools belong to many different denominations, which is the problem with counseling students. Christians in the school system should always show love to students. This will either reach those who don't know what love is or nurture those who do. Some schools prohibit signs of godliness or using the name Jesus on the grounds. Other schools allow teachers to advise students who wish to know more about Christ. As a result, some students have requested prayer, and some have confessed hope in Christ. It doesn't matter what the law says; Jesus can't truly be removed from schools. If there's a Christian on campus, Jesus is there. The dilemma is that unbelievers want the same rights to counsel students as Christians. The board of education won't allow only Christians to counsel students, and therefore Christians have to live as Christ to show children the way. Some children aren't seeking help because they've either never seen a real Christian, or they've been hurt by one. A man or woman who is a true representative of Christ will either draw these young people or turn them away. Being real and having a powerful prayer life is what children of all ages need. Whether we're working in a school or in a daycare, we are called to impart the Spirit of God. Leading people to Christ is the Great Commission.

Locally and nationwide, schools are blessed with teachers who have hearts for God and are passionate about saving souls. They work with their churches to help minister to teens, sometimes working with public programs authorized by school boards to teach children the basics of salvation with the parents' approval. A well-known example of such a program was developed by Tony Evans.

Over thirty years ago, a principal at a local Dallas high school contacted Tony Evans about an unusually high level of unrest at his school. At that time, the school was experiencing increased gang activity as well as other disruptive behaviors by students.

Dr. Evans responded to the call by sending twelve men to regularly walk the halls and restore order. Not only that, but he personally gathered all of the teen boys in the auditorium for a time to challenge them toward making right choices.

Before long, the school began to experience calm and stability. A change of atmosphere more conducive to learning emerged. Shortly after that, the principal was promoted to superintendent over a large cluster of schools and invited Dr. Evans and his church outreach ministry, now called The Turn•Around Agenda, to serve in all of the schools underneath his leadership. The social impact of this school intervention quickly spread to neighboring clusters as well. What began as a crisis intervention in one school has now become proactive intervention in over 52 public schools in Dallas County and parts of Fort Worth.

In 2006, The National Church Adopt-a-School Initiative was officially formed to both train and equip churches on how to replicate this proven model of social outreach in their area. NCAASI promotes community revitalization through church-based social services by leveraging the existing structures of both churches and schools (Evans, 2016).

Many churches have an evangelistic team going door to door and in the streets to spread the good news. NCAASI and other programs like it are like evangelistic teams for schools directed at teens. Whatever effective methods that are being used to win children to Christ are great. Teachers are in the forefront, but as parents, our primary responsibility is leading our children while supporting Christian teachers.

Summary

★ ★ ★ ★ ★ ★ ★ ★ ★

Greater love hath no man than this, that a man lay
down his life for his friends. (John 15:13)

★ ★ ★ ★ ★ ★ ★ ★ ★ ★

Jesus came to deliver us from captivity, so why are we choosing to be
in bondage? First, let us define biblical captivity. Perhaps it can be
defined as a mental prison, or a place with limited options. In Romans
7, Paul calls it a state of being trapped inside the body of death—having
the mind to serve God but a body warring against it to serve sin.

God has given humans the privilege of knowing love personally. To
know love is to be like love; being like love is sharing it with others.
Sharing love with others will prevent selfishness, judgment, and hateful
attitudes. A loving community of people shines a light for the entire
world to see that Jesus is the source of it, which will draw unbelievers
to him.

Love is an action word being played out by those who have agape
living within them. There are different types of love, but the kind of
love that leads to heaven is agape. Christians must stir up Jesus by
allowing God to operate freely within the body of Christ. The straight
and narrow path is an individual journey based on the freedom of
choice. No one can force a person to be real; God won't even force a
person to serve him. The gift of love was given to humans, but no one
is forced to take it. Jesus is the free gift, leaving us with the option of
receiving him or not.

To say "I'm a Christian" merely for recognition is living a lie. God wants honesty. Loving like God doesn't come by living without him. Loving God isn't hurting others. Loving God isn't about self-edification. God gave his only begotten Son for humankind's sake and for his glorification.

When people stop living on earth as if they are here to stay, giving freely to God will become easier. Unfortunately, the flesh is of the earth, and therefore it can become attached to the things that are here. When material things become more important than godly things, selfishness and hateful attitudes begin to play a role to prevent love from being seen. Christians can give more time to God, rather than to material things, by being spiritually minded.

Christians must take charge to allow love to be visible. Having material possession for enjoyment is okay, but once those things take priority over the Great Commission, we have a problem.

People are dying, but God has given the remedy to save them. For that husband, wife, sister, brother, cousin, uncle, and aunt; for that friend you've been praying for over the years; for that broken marriage or wayward child you've been fasting for; for the bedridden neighbor or the boss who's so hateful; for the prostitutes and drug addicts; and for the adulterers and compulsive liars—these people keep you on your knees, praying. Consider the leaders of the local assembly preying on single women with attempts to lower their value. The living word of God is saying, "If my people, which are called by my name, shall humble themselves, and pray, and seek my face, and turn from their wicked ways; then will I hear from heaven, and will forgive their sin, and will heal their land" (2 Chron. 7:14).

Some leaders proclaim to be men of God, but they're not knowledgeable enough to know that a woman of God can't lose her value. Christian women, it is up to you to carry yourselves as priceless jewels. But for men of God whom he made leaders in the church to view women in such a negative light, it shows just how much work needs to be done. We must reach not just those who are lost in the world, but those who are asleep in the house of God. "Turn from their wicked ways" (2 Chr. 7:14) is God's message for his people, so that he can attend unto the many prayers to heal the land.

When love is present, it invites peace, which creates a less stressful nation. The effect of love would cause employers to treat their employees fairly, people to give more freely to those in need, doctors to have better bedside manners, friends to hold true to the name, marriages to last, families to have stronger bonds, and saints to be on fire for the Lord. As a result, the world would be flabbergasted.

First things first. Let us start with the one in the mirror. We must learn what love is in every aspect of it. Breathe it, eat it, and revolve our whole lives around it. The power of love is how we will reach our homes, win our communities, and save a dying world. His grace is sufficient (2 Cor. 12:9).

Testimonial

During my preteen years, I had a huge crush on a boy in high school. At the time, I felt that it was love. I thought about him all the time—when I awakened in the morning, throughout the day, and before I went to bed. One day I was standing in my parents' yard, and I saw him drive by. I waved at him with so much joy because seeing him was the highlight of my day. After he drove by, I looked up at the sky and thought, *God, I want to love you like that.*

Immediately, the enemy said, "You can't love God like that. He is in heaven." I slowly turned and walked back inside the house, but my heart still desired to be close to God.

I grew up in a small town, and my church only met on the fourth Sunday of each month. Sometimes we'd attend other churches, but other times we stayed at home. One Sunday morning I was standing in my doorway, and a family passed by on their way to church. When I saw them, I made a promise to myself within my heart. *When I'm an adult, I'm going to church every Sunday.*

I believe with all my heart that God heard me, because today he is my first thought of the day, he is on my mind all day long, and he is my last thought before I go to sleep at night. He has led me to a church with a pastor who loves the Lord. At this point of my life, I seek to know him more so that I can hear him better to have a closer walk with him. Does this mean that I am perfect? No, but it does mean that I seek after perfection to be more like Jesus, who died and gave himself for me as he did for you.

Scripture Referenced, KJV

1 Corinthians 2:4–5. And my speech and my preaching was not with enticing words of man's wisdom, but in demonstration of the Spirit and of power: That your faith should not stand in the wisdom of men, but in the power of God.

1 Corinthians 3:7. So then neither is he that planteth any thing, neither he that watereth; but God that giveth the increase.

1 Corinthians 6:17. Flee fornication. Every sin that a man doeth is without the body; but he that committeth fornication sinneth against his own body.

1 Corinthian 6:19. Know ye not that your body is the temple of the Holy Spirit which is in you, which ye have of God, and ye are not your own?

1 Corinthians 6:20. For ye are bought with a price: therefore glorify God in your body, and in your spirit, which are God's.

1 Corinthians 7:5. Defraud ye not one the other, except it be with consent for a time, that ye may give yourselves to fasting and prayer; and come together again, that Satan tempt you not for your incontinency.

1 Corinthians 7:22. For he that is called in the Lord, being a servant, is the Lord's freeman: likewise also he that is called, being free, is Christ's servant.

1 Corinthians 7:24. Brethren, let every man, wherein he is called, therein abide with God.

1 Corinthians 10:8. Neither let us commit fornication, as some of them committed, and fell in one day three and twenty thousand.

1 Corinthians 10:9. Neither let us tempt Christ, as some of them also tempted, and were destroyed of serpents.

1 Corinthians 11:31. For if we judge ourselves, we should not be judged.

1 Corinthians 13:4–8. Charity suffereth long, and is kind; love envieth not; love vaunteth not itself, it not puffed up, Doth not behave itself unseemly, seeketh not her own, is not easily provoked, thinketh no evil; Rejoiceth not in iniquity, but rejoiceth in the truth; Beareth all things, believeth all things, hopeth all things, endureth all things. Charity never faileth.

1 Corinthians 15:58. Therefore, my beloved brethren, be ye stedfast, unmovable, always abounding in the work of the Lord, forasmuch as ye know that your labour is not in vain in the Lord.

1 John 2:15. Love not the world, neither the things that are in the world. If any man love the world, the love of the Father is not in him.

1 John 2:16. For all that is in the world, the lust of the flesh, and the lust of the eyes, and the pride of life, is not of the Father, but is of the world.

1 John 3:14. We know that we have passed from death unto life, because we love the brethren. He that loveth not his brother abideth in death.

1 John 3:18. Let us not love in word, neither in tongue; but in deed and in truth.

1 John 4:7. Let us love one another: for love is of God; and every one that loveth is born of God, and knoweth God.

1 John 4:8. He that loveth not knoweth not God; for God is love.

1 John 4:12–13. If we love one another, God dwelleth in us, and his love is perfected in us. Hereby know we that we dwell in him, and he in us, because he hath given us of his Spirit.

1 John 4:16. And we have known and believed the love that God hath to us. God is love; and he that dwelleth in love dwelleth in God, and God in him.

1 John 4:20. If a man say, I love God, and hateth his brother, he is a liar: for he that loveth not his brother whom he hath seen, how can he love God whom he hath not seen?

1 John 5:14. And this is the confidence that we have in him, that, if we ask any thing according to his will, he heareth us:

1 Kings 2:12. Then sat Solomon upon the throne of David his father; and his kingdom was established greatly.

1 Kings 4:29–34. And God gave Solomon wisdom and understanding exceeding much and largeness of heart, even as the sand that is on the sea shore. And Solomon's wisdom excelled the wisdom of all the children of the east country, and all the wisdom of Egypt. For he was wiser than all men; than Ethan the Ezrahite, and Heman, and Chalcol, and Darda, and sons of Mahol: and his fame was in all nations round about. And he spake three thousand proverbs: and his songs were a thousand and five. And he spake of trees, from the cedar tree that is in Lebanon even unto the hyssop that springeth out of the wall: he spake also of beasts, and of fowl, and of creeping things, and of fishes. And there came of all people to hear the wisdom of Solomon, from all kings of the earth, which had heard of his wisdom.

1 Kings 11:3. And he had seven hundred wives, princesses, and three hundred concubines: and his wives turned away his heart.

1 Peter 2:2. As newborn babes, desires the sincere milk of the word, that ye may grow thereby:

1 Peter 2:9. Ye are a chosen generation, a royal priesthood, an holy nation, a peculiar people; that ye should shew forth the praises of him who hath called you out of darkness into his marvelous light.

1 Peter 2:13. Submit yourselves to every ordinance of man for the Lord's sake: whether it be to the king, as supreme;

1 Peter 2:21. For even hereunto were ye called: because Christ also suffered for us, leaving us an example, that ye should follow his steps:

1 Peter 4:8–9. And above all things have fervent charity among yourselves: for charity shall cover the multitude of sins. Use hospitality one to another without grudging.

1 Peter 5:8. Be sober, be vigilant; because your adversary the devil, as a roaring lion, walketh about, seeking whom he may devour.

1 Thessalonians 4:16–18. For the Lord himself shall descend from heaven with a shout, with the voice of the archangel, and with the trump of God: and the dead in Christ shall rise first: Then we which are alive and remain shall be caught up together with them in the clouds, to meet the Lord in the air: and so shall we ever be with the Lord. Wherefore comfort one another with these words.

1 Thessalonians 5:6. Therefor let us not sleep, as do others; but let us watch and be sober.

1 Thessalonians 5:8. But let us, who are of the day, be sober, putting on the breastplate of faith and love; and for an helmet, the hope of salvation.

1 Timothy 4:14. Neglect not the gift that is in thee, which was given thee by prophecy, with the laying on of the hands of the presbytery.

1 Timothy 6:8. And having food and raiment let us therefore be content.

1 Timothy 6:9. But they that will be rich fall into temptation and a snare, and into many foolish and hurtful lusts, which drown men in destruction and perdition. For the love of money is the root of all evil: which while some coveted after, they have erred from the faith, and pierced themselves through with many sorrows.

1 Timothy 6:12. Fight the good fight of faith, lay hold on eternal life, whereunto thou art also called, and hast professed a good profession before many witnesses.

2 Chronicles 7:14. If my people, which are called by my name, shall humble themselves, and pray, and seek my face, and turn from their wicked ways; then will I hear from heaven, and will forgive their sin, and will heal their land.

2 Corinthians 2:10–11. To whom ye forgive any thing, I forgive also: for if I forgave any thing, to whom I forgave it, for your sakes forgave I it in the person of Christ; Lest Satan should get an advantage of us: for we are not ignorant of his devices.

2 Corinthians 4:3–4. If our gospel be hid, it is hid to them that are lost. In whom the god of this world hath blinded the minds of them which believe not, lest the light of the glorious gospel of Christ, who is the image of God, should shine unto them.

2 Corinthians 5:17. Therefore if any man be in Christ, he is a new creature: old things are passed away; behold, all things are become new.

2 Corinthians 5:18. And all things are of God, who hath reconciled us to himself by Jesus Christ, and hath given to us the ministry of reconciliation

2 Corinthians 5:20. Now then we are ambassadors for Christ, as though God did beseech you by us: we pray you in Christ's stead, be ye reconciled to God.

2 Corinthians 7:1. Let us cleanse ourselves from all filthiness of the flesh and spirit, perfecting holiness in the fear of God.

2 Corinthians 10:5. Casting down imaginations, and every high thing that exalteth itself against the knowledge of God, and bringing into captivity every thought to the obedience of Christ.

2 Corinthians 12:9. And he said unto me, My grace is sufficient for thee: for my strength is made perfect in weakness. Most gladly therefore, will I rather glory in my infirmities, that the power of Christ may rest upon me.

2 Corinthians 13:5. Examine yourselves, whether ye be in the faith; prove your own selves. Know ye not your own selves, how that Jesus Christ is in you, except ye be reprobates?

2 Peter 1:3. God hath given unto us all things that pertain unto life and godliness, through the knowledge of him that hath called us to glory and virtue.

2 Peter 1:5–7. Add to your faith virtue; and to virtue knowledge; and to knowledge temperance; and to temperance patience; and to patience godliness; and to godliness brotherly kindness; and brotherly kindness charity. He went on to say in verse eight ... if these things be in you, and abound, they make you that ye shall neither be barren nor unfruitful in the knowledge of our Lord Jesus Christ.

2 Peter 1:9–10. But he that lacketh these things is blind, and cannot see afar off, and hath forgotten that he was purged from his old sins. Wherefore the rather, brethren, give diligence to make your calling and election sure.

2 Peter 1:21. For the prophecy came not in old time by the will of man: but holy men of God spake as they were moved by the Holy Ghost.

2 Peter 2:6. Turning the cities of Sodom and Gomorrah into ashes condemned them with an overthrow, making them an ensample into those that after should live ungodly.

2 Peter 3:1–2. I now write unto you; in (first & second epistle) both which I stir up your pure minds by way of remembrance: That ye may be mindful of the words which were spoken before by the holy prophets and of the commandment of the apostles of the Lord and Saviour.

2 Peter 3:9. The Lord is not slack concerning his promise, as some men count slackness; but is longsuffering to us-ward, not willing that any should perish, but that all should come to repentance.

2 Samuel 12:13. And David said unto Nathan, I have sinned against the LORD. And Nathan said unto David, The LORD also hath put away thy sin; thou shalt not die.

2 Thessalonians 3:13–15. And if any man obey not our word by this epistle, note that man, and have no company with him, that he may be ashamed. Yet count him not an enemy, but admonish him as a brother.

2 Timothy 1:6. Wherefore I put thee in remembrance that thou stir up the gift of God, which is in thee which is in thee by the putting on of my hands.

2 Timothy 1:9. Who hath saved us, and called us with an holy calling, not according to our works, but according to his own purpose and grace, which was given us in Christ Jesus before the world began.

2 Timothy 2:19. Nevertheless the foundation of God standeth sure, having this seal, The Lord knoweth them that are his. And, Let every one that nameth the name of Christ depart from iniquity.

2 Timothy 2:21. If man therefore purge himself from these he shall be a vessel unto honour, sanctified, and meet [fit] for the master's use, and prepared unto every good work.

2 Timothy 3:1. This know also, that in the last days perilous times shall come.

2 Timothy 3:5. Having a form of godliness but denying the power thereof: from such turn away.

2 Timothy 4:3. For there will come a time when they will not endure sound doctrine; but after their own lusts shall they heap to themselves teachers, having itching ears

Acts 2:38. Repent, and be baptized every one of you in the name of Jesus Christ for the remission of sins, and ye shall receive the gift of the Holy Ghost.

Acts 5:29. Then Peter and the other apostles answered and said, We ought to obey God rather than men.

Acts 13:9. Then Saul, (who also is called Paul,) filled with the Holy Ghost, set his eyes on him.

Acts 13:22. And when he had removed him, he raised up unto them David to be their king; to whom also he gave testimony, and said, I have found David the son of Jesse, a man after mine own heart, which shall fulfill all my will.

Acts 16:30. And brought them out, and said, Sirs, what must I do to be saved?

Acts 17:28. For in him we live, and move, and have our being; as certain also of your own poets have said, For we are also his offspring.

Acts 20:35. I have shewed you all things, how that so labouring ye ought to support the weak, and to remember the words of the Lord Jesus, how he said, It is more blessed to give than to receive.

Colossians 3:15. let the peace of God rule in your hearts, to the which also ye are called in one body; and be ye thankful.

Colossians 3:22–23. Servants, obey in all things your masters according to the flesh; not with eyeservice, as menpleasers; but in singleness of heart, fearing God: And whatsoever ye do, do it heartily, as to the Lord, and not unto men.

Ephesians 1:7. I have redemption through his blood, the forgiveness of sins, according to the riches of his grace

Ephesians 1:13. In whom I also trusted, after that I heard the word of truth, the gospel of my salvation: in whom also after that I believed, I was sealed with the Holy Spirit of promise.

Ephesians 2:10. For we are his workmanship, created in Christ Jesus unto good works, which God hath before ordained that we should walk in them.

Ephesians 4:16. From whom the whole body fitly joined together and compacted by that which every joint supplieth, according to the effectual working in the measure of every part, maketh increase of the body unto the edifying of itself in love.

Ephesians 4:29. No corrupt communication proceed out of your mouth, but that which is good to the use of edifying, that is may minister grace unto the hearers.

Ephesians 4:30. And grieve not the holy Spirit of God, whereby ye are sealed unto the day of redemption.

Ephesians 5:22. Wives, submit yourselves unto your own husbands, as unto the Lord.

Ephesians 5:25. Husbands, love our wives, even as Christ also loved the church, and gave himself for it

Ephesians 6:12. For we wrestle not against flesh and blood, but against principalities, against powers, against the rulers of the darkness of this world, against spiritual wickedness in high places.

Ephesians 6:13. Wherefore take unto you the whole armour of God, that ye may be able to withstand in the evil day, and having done all, to stand.

Ephesians 6:15. And your feet shod with the preparation of the gospel of peace

Exodus 2:11–12. And it came to pass in those days, when Moses was grown, that he went out unto his brethren: and he spied an Egyptian smiting an Hebrew, one of his brethren. And he looked this way and that way, and when he saw that there was no man, he slew the Egyptian, and hid him in the sand.

Galatians 1:10. For do I now persuade men, or God? Or do I seek to please men? for if I yet pleased men, I should not be the servant of Christ.

Galatians 5:1. Stand fast therefore in the liberty wherewith Christ hath made us free, and be not entangled again with the yoke of bondage.

Galatians 5:16–17. Walk in the Spirit, and ye shall not fulfill the lust of the flesh. For the flesh lusteth against the Spirit, and the Spirit against the flesh.

Galatians 5:22–23. But the fruit of the Spirit is love, joy, peace, longsuffering, gentleness, goodness, faith, Meekness, temperance: against such there is no law.

Galatians 5:25. If we live in the Spirit, let us also walk in the Spirit.

Galatians 5:26. Let us not be desirous of vain glory, provoking one another, envying one another.

Galatians 6:9. Let us not be weary in well doing: for in due season we shall reap, if we faint not.

Galatians 6:10. As we have therefore opportunity, let us do good unto all men, especially unto them who are of the household of faith.

Genesis 2:7. And the LORD God formed man of the dust of the ground, and breathed into his nostrils the breath of life; and man became of living soul.

Genesis 14:22. And Abram said to the king of Sodom, I have lift up mine hand unto the LORD, the most high God, the possessor of heaven and earth.

Hebrews 4:12. For the word of God is quick, and powerful, and sharper than any twoedged sword, piercing even to the dividing asunder of soul and spirit, and of the joints and marrow, and is a discerner of the thoughts and intents of the heart.

Hebrews 4:14. Seeing then that we have a great high priest, that is passed into the heavens, Jesus the Son of God, let us hold fast our profession.

Hebrews 4:16. Let us therefore come boldly unto the throne of grace, that we may obtain mercy, and find grace to help in time of need.

Hebrews 6:4. For it is impossible for those who were once enlightened, and have tasted the heavenly gift, and were made partakers of the Holy Ghost, And have tasted the good word of God, and the powers of the world to come, If they shall fall away, to renew them again unto repentance.

Hebrews 6:6. If they shall fall away, to renew them again unto repentance; seeing they crucify to themselves the Son of God afresh, and put him to an open shame.

Hebrews 6:18–19. That by two immutable things, in which it was impossible for God to lie, we might have a strong consolation, who have fled for refuge to lay hold upon the hope set before us: 19Which hope we have as an anchor of the soul, both sure and stedfast, and which entereth into that within the veil.

Hebrews 10:23. Let us hold fast the profession of our faith without wavering; (for he is faithful that promised;)

Hebrews 10:25. Not forsaking the assembling of ourselves together, as the manner of some is; but exhorting one another: and so much the more, as ye see the day approaching.

Hebrews 11:6. Without faith it is impossible to please him: for he that cometh to God must believe that he is, and that he is a rewarder of them that diligently seek him.

Hebrews 12:1–2. Wherefore seeing we also are compassed about with so great a cloud of witnesses, let us lay aside every weight, and the sin which doth so easily beset us, and let us run with patience the race that is set before us, 2Looking unto Jesus the author and finisher of our faith; who for the joy that was set before him endured the cross, despising the shame, and is set down at the right hand of the throne of God.

Hebrews 12:15. Looking diligently lest any man fail of the grace of God; lest any root of bitterness springing up trouble you, and thereby many be defiled

Hebrews 12:28. Wherefore we receiving a kingdom which cannot be moved, let us have grace, whereby we may serve God acceptably with reverence and godly fear.

Hebrews 13:4. Marriage is honourable in all, and the bed undefiled: but whoremongers and adulterers God will judge.

Hebrews 13:5. I give unto them eternal life; and they shall never perish, neither shall any man pluck them out of my hand. John 10:28. I will never leave thee, nor forsake thee.

Hebrews 13:15. By him therefore let us offer the sacrifice of praise to God continually, that is, the fruit of our lips giving thanks to his name.

Isaiah 9:6. For unto us a child is born, unto us a son is given: and the government shall be upon his shoulder: and his name shall be called Wonderful, Counsellor, The mighty God, The everlasting Father, The Prince of Peace.

Isaiah 41:10. Fear thou not; for I am with thee: be not dismayed; for I am thy God: I will strengthen thee; yea, I will help thee; yea, I will uphold thee with the right hand of my righteousness.

Isaiah 43:2. When thou passest through the waters, I will be with thee; and through the rivers, they shall not overflow thee: when thou walkest through the fire, thou shalt not be burned; neither shall the flame kindle upon thee.

Isaiah 55:8. For my thoughts are not your thoughts, neither are your ways my ways, saith the LORD.

Isaiah 55:11. So shall my word be that goeth forth out of my mouth: it shall not return unto me void, but it shall accomplish that which I please, and it shall prosper in the thing whereto I sent it.

James 1:20. For the wrath of man worketh not the righteousness of God.

James 1:23–24. For if any be a hearer of the word, and not a doer, he is like unto a man beholding his natural face in a glass: For he beholdeth himself, and goeth his way, and straightway forgetteth what manner of man he was.

James 1:26. If any man among you seem to be religious, and bridleth not his tongue, but deceiveth his own heart, this man religion is vain.

James 3:10. Out of the same mouth proceedeth blessing and cursing. My brethren, these things ought not so to be.

James 3:8. But the tongue can no man tame; it is an unruly evil, full of deadly poison.

James 4:11. Speak not evil one of another, brethren. He that speaketh evil of his brother, and judgeth his brother, speaketh evil of the law, and judgeth the law: but if thou judge the law, thou art not a doer of the law, but a judge.

James 5:15. And the prayer of faith shall save the sick, and the Lord shall raise him up; and if he have committed sins, they shall be forgiven him.

John 3:6. That which is born of the flesh is flesh and that which is born of the Spirit is spirit.

John 3:16. God so loved the world, that he gave his only begotten Son, that whosoever believeth in him should not perish, but have everlasting life.

John 3:17. For God sent not his Son into the world to condemn the world; but that the world through him might be saved.

John 4:23–24. But the hour cometh, and now is, when the true worshippers shall worship the Father in spirit and in truth: for the Father seeketh such to worship him. God is a Spirit and they that worship him must worship him in spirit and in truth.

John 8:12. Then spake Jesus again unto them, saying, I am the light of the world: he that followeth me shall not walk in darkness, but shall have the light of life.

John 8:36. If the Son therefore shall make you free, ye shall be free indeed.

John 9:4. I must work the works of him that sent me, while it is day: the night cometh, when no man can work.

John 10:10. The thief cometh not, but for to steal, and to kill, and to destroy: I am come that they might have life, and that they might have it more abundantly.

John 13:34. A new commandment I give unto you, That ye love one another; as I have loved you, that ye also love one another.

John 14:7. If ye abide in me, and my words abide in you, ye shall ask what ye will, and it shall be done unto you.

John 14:12. Verily, verily, I say unto you, He that believeth on me, the works that I do shall he do also; and greater works than these shall he do.

John 14:27. Peace I leave with you, my peace I give unto you: not as the world giveth, give I unto you. Let not your heart be troubled, neither let it be afraid.

John 15:5. I am the vine, ye are the branches: He that abideth in me, and I in him, the same bringeth forth much fruit: for without me ye can do nothing.

John 16:13. Howbeit when he the Spirit of truth, is come, he will guide you into the truth: for he shall not speak of himself; but whatsoever he shall hear, that shall he speak: and he will shew you things to come.

John 17:13–20. And now come I to thee and these things I speak in the world, that they might have my joy fulfilled in themselves. I have given them they world; and the world hath hated them, because they are not of the world, even as I am not of the world. I pray not that thou shouldest take them out of the world, but that thou shouldest keep them from the evil. They are not of the world, even as I am not of the world, even as I am not of the world. Sanctify them through thy truth: thy word is truth. As thou hast sent me into the world, even so have I also sent them into the world. And for their sakes I sanctify myself, that they also might be sanctified through the truth. Neither pray I for these alone, but for them also which shall believe on me through their word.

Jonah 1:1–2. Now the word of the LORD came unto Johan … Arise, go to Nineveh, that great city, and cry against it; for their wickedness is come up before me. But Jonah rose up to flee unto Tarshish form the presence of the LORD.

Jude 1:20–23. Building up yourselves on you most holy faith, praying in the Holy Ghost, Keep yourselves in the love of God, looking for the mercy of our Lord Jesus Christ unto eternal life. And of some have compassion, making a difference: And others save with fear, pulling (snatching) them out of the fire; hating even the garment spotted by flesh.

Jude 1:24–25. Now unto him that is able to keep you from falling, and to present you faultless before the presence of his glory with exceeding joy, To the only wise God our Saviour, be glory and majesty, dominion and power, both now and forever. Amen.

Leviticus 20:13. If a man also lie with mankind, as he lieth with a woman, both of them have committed an abomination: they shall surely be put to death; their blood shall be upon them.

Luke 9:23. And he said to them all, If any man will come after me, let him deny himself, and take up his cross daily, and follow me.

Luke 15:4. Having an hundred sheep, if he lost one of them, doth not leave the ninety and nine in the wilderness, and go after that which is lost, until he find it?

Luke 22:42. Saying, Father, if thou be willing, remove this cup from me: nevertheless not my will, but thine, be done.

Mark 13:32. But of that day and that hour knoweth no man, no, not the angels which are in heaven, neither the Son, but the Father.

Matthew 4:17. From that time Jesus began to preach, and to say, Repent: for the kingdom of heaven is at hand.

Matthew 5:11. Blessed are ye, when men shall revile you, and persecute you, and shall say all manner of evil against you falsely, for my sake.

Matthew 5:13. Ye are the salt of the earth: but if the salt have lost his savour, wherewith shall it be salted? It is thenceforth good for nothing.

Matthew 5:14. Ye are the light of the world. A city that is set on an hill cannot be hid.

Matthew 5:16. Let your light so shine before men, that they may see your good works, and glorify your Father which is in heaven.

Matthew 5:44. I say unto you, Love your enemies, bless them that curse you, do good to them that hate you, and pray for them which despitefully use you, and persecute you.

Matthew 6:7. But when ye pray use not vain repetitions, as the heathen do: for they think that they shall be heard for their much speaking.

Matthew 6:15. If ye forgive not men their trespasses, neither will your Father forgive your trespasses.

Matthew 7:1. Judge not, that ye be not judged.

Matthew 7:3. And why beholdest thou the mote [speck] that is in thy brother's eye, but considerest not the beam [large wood] that is in thine own eye?

Matthew 7:16. Ye shall know them by their fruits. Do men gather grapes of thorns, or figs of thistles?

Matthew 11:29. Take my yoke upon you, and learn of me; for I am meek and lowly in heart: and ye shall find rest unto your souls.

Matthew 16:24. If any man will come after me, let him deny himself, and take up his cross, and follow me.

Matthew 18:15. If they brother shall trespass (sin) against thee, go and tell him his fault between thee and him alone.

Matthew 19:4. He which made them at the beginning made them male and female.

Numbers 23:19. God is not a man that he should lie; neither the son of man, that he should repent: hath he said, and shall he not do it? or hath he spoken, and shall he not make it good?

Philippians 2:12. Wherefore, my beloved, as ye have always obeyed, not as in my presence only, but now much more in my absence, work out your own salvation with fear and trembling.

Philippians 2:13. For it is God [Elohim in Spirit] which worketh in you both to will and to do of his good pleasure.

Philippians 3:14. I press toward the mark for the prize of the high calling of God in Christ Jesus.

Philippians 4:1. Therefore, my brethren dearly beloved and longed for, my joy and crown, so stand fast in the Lord, my dearly beloved.

Philippians 4:4–7. Rejoice in the Lord alway: and again I say, Rejoice. Let your moderation be known unto all men. The Lord is at hand. Be careful for nothing; but in every thing by prayer and supplication with thanksgiving let your requests be made known unto God. And the peace of God, which passeth all understanding, shall keep your hearts and minds through Christ Jesus.

Philippians 4:8. Finally, brethren, whatsoever things are true, whatsoever things are honest, whatsoever things are just, whatsoever things are pure, whatsoever things are lovely, whatsoever things are of good report; if there be any virtue, and if there be any praise, think on these things.

Philippians 4:19. But my God shall supply all your need according to his riches in glory by Christ Jesus.

Proverbs 10:19. In a multitude of words there wanteth not sin: but he that refraineth his lips is wise.

Proverbs 13:24. He that spareth his rod hateth his son: but he that loveth him chasteneth him betimes.

Proverbs 15:1–2. A soft answer turneth away wrath: but grievous words stir up anger. The tongue of the wise useth knowledge aright: but the mouth of fools poureth out foolishness.

Proverbs 17:17. A friend loveth at all times, and a brother is born for adversity.

Proverbs 18:24. A man that hath friends must shew himself friendly: and there is a friend that sticketh closer than a brother.

Proverbs 22:6. Train up a child in the way he should go: and when he is old, he will not depart from it.

Proverbs 23:7. For as he thinketh in his heart, so is he: Eat and drink, saith he to thee; but his heart is not with thee.

Proverbs 27:17. Iron sharpeneth iron; so a man sharpeneth the countenance of his friend.

Psalm 1:1. Blessed is the man that walketh not in the counsel of the ungodly, nor standeth in the way of sinners, nor sitteth in the set of the scornful.

Psalm 18:3. I will call upon the LORD, who is worthy to be praised: so shall I be saved from mine enemies.

Psalm 23:3. He restoreth my soul: he leadeth me in the paths of righteousness for his name's sake.

Psalm 24:1. The earth is the LORD's, and the fullness thereof; the world, and they that dwell therein.

Psalm 27:1. The LORD is my light and my salvation; whom shall I fear? the LORD is the strength of my life; of whom shall I be afraid?

Psalm 139:23–24. Search me, O God, and know my heart: try me, and know my thoughts: And see if there be any wicked way in me, and lead me in the way everlasting.

Revelation 1:8. I am Alpha and Omega, the beginning and the ending, saith the Lord, which is, and which was, and which is to come, the Almighty.

Revelation 3:19. As many as I love, I rebuke and chasten: be zealous therefore, and repent.

Revelation 19:7. Let us be glad and rejoice, and give honour to him: for the marriage of the Lamb is come, and his wife hath made herself ready.

Romans 1:24–28. Wherefore God also gave them up to uncleanness through the lusts of their own hearts, to dishonor their own bodies between themselves: Who changed the truth of God into a lie, and worshipped and served the creature more than the Creator, who is blessed for ever. Amen. For this cause God gave them up unto vile affections: for even their women did change the natural use into that which is against nature: And likewise also the men, leaving the natural use of the woman, burned in their lust one toward another; men with men working that which is unseemly, and receiving in themselves that recompence of their error which was meet. And even as they did not like to retain God in their knowledge, God gave them over to a reprobate mind, to do those things which are not convenient.

Romans 2:1. Therefore thou art inexcusable, O man, whosoever thou art that judgest: for wherein thou judgest another, thou condemnest thyself; for thou that judgest doest the same things.

Romans 6:23. For the wages of sin is death; but the gift of God is eternal life through Jesus Christ our Lord.

Romans 8:4. That the righteousness of the law might be fulfilled in us, who walk not after the flesh, but after the Spirit.

Romans 8:9. But ye are not in the flesh, but in the Spirit, if so be that the Spirit of God dwell in you. Now if any man have not the Spirit of Christ, he is none of his.

Romans 8:24–25. For we are saved by hope: but hope that is seen is not hope: for what a man seeth, why doth he yet hope for? But if we hope for that we see not, then do we with patience wait for it.

Romans 8:31. What shall we say to these things? If God be for us, who can be against us?

Romans 8:36. As it is written, For thy sake we are killed all the day long; we are accounted as sheep for the slaughter.

Romans 8:37. Nay, in all these things we are more than conquerors through him that loved us.

Romans 10:13. For whosoever shall call upon the name of the Lord shall be saved.

Romans 12:2. Be ye transformed by the renewing of your mind, that ye may prove what is that good, and acceptable, and perfect, will of God.

Romans 12:4–6. For as we have many members in one body, and all members have not the same office: So we, being many, are one body in Christ, and every one members one to another. Having then gifts differing according to the grace that is given to us.

Romans 12:19. Dearly beloved, avenge not yourselves, but rather give place unto wrath: for it is written, Vengeance is mine; I will repay, saith the Lord.

Romans 13:8. Owe no man any thing, but to love one another: for he that loveth another hath fulfilled the law.

Romans 13:9. Thou shalt not commit adultery, Thou shalt not kill, Thou shalt not steal, Thou shalt not bear false witness, Thou shalt not covet; and if there be any other commandment, it is briefly comprehended in this saying, namely, Thou shalt love thy neighbor as thyself.

Romans 13:11. And that, Knowing the time, that now it is high time to awake out of sleep: for now is our salvation nearer than when we believed.

Romans 13:12. The night is far spent, the day is at hand: let us therefore cast off the works of darkness, and let us put on the armour of light.

Romans 13:14. Let us walk honestly, as in the day; not in rioting and drunkenness, not in chambering and wantonness, not in strife and envying.

Romans 14:13. Let us not therefore judge one another any more: but judge this rather, that no man put a stumblingblock or an occasion to fall in his brother's way.

Romans 14:19. Let us therefore follow after the things which make for peace, and things wherewith one may edify another.

Titus 2:13. Looking for that blessed hope, and the glorious appearing of the great God and our Saviour Jesus Christ (The Holy Bible, 2007).

Beers. (1996). Touch Point Bible. In R. a. Beers, *Touch Point Bible: New Living Translation* (p. 1196). Wheaton: Tyndale.

Evans, D. T. (2016, April 18). *A DIVISION OF THE URBAN ALTERNATIVE WITH DR. TONY EVANS*. Retrieved from The National Church Adopt A School Initiative: http://churchadoptaschool. org/about-the-national-church-adopt-a-school-initiative/

Henry, M. (1991). Matthew Henry, Matthew Henry's Commentary on the Whole Bible. In M. Henry, *Matthew Henry, Matthew Henry's Commentary on the Whole Bible complete and unabridged in one volume* (pp. 816-817). Peabody: Hendrickson Publishers, LLC.

Murnaghan, I. (2017, July 14). *Stem Cells and Same Sex Reproduction*. Retrieved from Explore Stem Cell: http://www.explorestemcells. co.uk/stem-cells-same-sex-reproduction.html

The Holy Bible, K. J. (2007, November). *King James Bible Online*. Retrieved from King James Bible (KJV). www.kingjamesbibleonline.org

About the Author

Elnora Wilson was born and raised in Uniontown, Alabama. Before she started writing informative books, most of her time was spent being a full time mother of three.

Her first book, *Youth Ministries: Sexual Purity*, encouraged teenagers and young adults to live by Christian morals. All of her writings are driven by her passion to use her spiritual gifts and talents to encourage the body of Christ to love one another according to the word of God.

Printed in the United States
By Bookmasters